Why Aren't You Writing?

This one goes out to all the struggling writers out there.

Sara Miller McCune founded SAGE Publishing in 1965 to support the dissemination of usable knowledge and educate a global community. SAGE publishes more than 1000 journals and over 800 new books each year, spanning a wide range of subject areas. Our growing selection of library products includes archives, data, case studies and video. SAGE remains majority owned by our founder and after her lifetime will become owned by a charitable trust that secures the company's continued independence.

Los Angeles | London | New Delhi | Singapore | Washington DC | Melbourne

Why Aren't You Writing?

Research, Real Talk, Strategies, and Shenanigans

Sharon Zumbrunn
Virginia Commonwealth University

Los Angeles | London | New Delhi
Singapore | Washington DC | Melbourne

FOR INFORMATION:

SAGE Publications, Inc.
2455 Teller Road
Thousand Oaks, California 91320
E-mail: order@sagepub.com

SAGE Publications Ltd.
1 Oliver's Yard
55 City Road
London, EC1Y 1SP
United Kingdom

SAGE Publications India Pvt. Ltd.
B 1/I 1 Mohan Cooperative Industrial Area
Mathura Road, New Delhi 110 044
India

SAGE Publications Asia-Pacific Pte. Ltd.
18 Cross Street #10-10/11/12
China Square Central
Singapore 048423

Printed in Canada

ISBN 978-1-5443-4115-6

This book is printed on acid-free paper.

Acquisitions Editor: Leah Fargotstein
Editorial Assistant: Kelsey Barkis
Production Editor: Gagan Mahindra
Copy Editor: Exeter Premedia Services
Typesetter: Exeter Premedia Services
Proofreader: Ellen Brink
Cover Designer: Scott Van Atta
Marketing Manager: Victoria Velasquez

MIX
Paper from
responsible sources
FSC® C103567

20 21 22 23 24 10 9 8 7 6 5 4 3 2 1

Brief Contents

Detailed Contents

Chapter 4 Writing Self-Efficacy 45

Acknowledgments

I feel lucky to have had the opportunity to write this book and I'm thankful for the many colleagues, friends, and family members who helped make it happen. First, thank you to my husband and two littles for their encouragement throughout this project ("Mommy, are you ever going to be done with your book?"). A special thanks to my editor, Leah Fargotstein, for always believing in this work, making it better, and not even hinting once that you wanted to break up with me. Jenna Furman, my ride-or-die on this project, thanks for being the most amazing assistant. Your huge brain helped me puzzle through so many of the challenges and your constant positive spirit and grace no doubt kept me afloat. Thank you also to Preeti Kamat who helped with the early research for this book. Sarah Marrs, my writing wing-woman, thank you for always being willing to let me borrow your brain when I am stuck. I feel lucky to have found someone who understands and willingly accepts all of my shenanigans. Eric Ekholm, your hilarious ideas and close eye for detail helped make this book real—thank you for both your red pen and your wit. Christine Bae, Chelsi Klentz-Davis, Carlton Fong, Philip Gnilka, Kathy Rudasill, Genevieve Siegel-Hawley, Ashley Vaughn, and members of my research lab, thank you for the generous and kind feedback that both hugged my heart and improved the writing throughout this project. To Lou and the rest of my fam, thank you for being so excited about this work. Thank you also to Roger Bruning for inspiring my love of writing research and to Beth Doll for being the namesake for this book (see strategies, Chapter 3). Finally, I'm especially thankful to the many academic writers who have vulnerably shared their experiences and who have made me feel more normal about my own writing neuroses in the process.

SAGE and the author would like to thank the following reviewers for their comments throughout the development process:

Michael Cox, Ohio Christian University

Thomas Deluca, University of Kansas

Alejandra Dubois, University of Ottawa

Octavio Esqueda, Biola University

Leigh Falls, University of Memphis

Holly C. Gould, University of Lynchburg

Anne Hacker, Walden University

Stacy Haynes, Mississippi State University

Caitlin M. Lapine, SUNY Old Westbury

Nils Myszkowski, Pace University

Miriam Northcutt Bohmert, Indiana University Bloomington

Huma Shah, Loma Linda University

Leane Skinner, Auburn University

About the Author

Sharon Zumbrunn is an independent coach, as well as an associate professor of educational psychology and the co-director of the Motivation in Context Research Lab at Virginia Commonwealth University. As a feelings-and-learning-ologist, she spends a whole lot of time thinking about and studying writing motivation and self-regulation. She has published several research articles on the writing context, writing self-efficacy, writing attitudes, perceptions of feedback, and writing strategies. Importantly, she self-identifies as a struggling writer . . . depending on the day. She currently resides with her husband, two kids, charming-but-annoying dog, and hordes of woodland creatures in Charlottesville, Virginia. Learn more at sharonzumbrunn.com or follow her on Twitter (@SharonZumbrunn) and Instagram (@SZumbrunn).

Introduction

This is how you do it: you sit down at the keyboard and you put one word after another until it's done. It's that easy, and that hard.

—**Neil Gaiman**

Ugh. You ain't lying, Neil. Writing *is* tough. As the universe would have it, here I am truly struggling with writing the introduction to this book and feeling slightly triggered by its title.[1] I've started and stalled out at least a dozen times. Though the irony here is thick, it's a sort of irony that I'm unfortunately somewhat used to as someone who studies the development of writing motivation and productivity and as someone who also happens to identify as a struggling writer. Writing just happens to be a complex cognitive and motivational process that makes most writers—even really good writers and super bright people with PhDs—feel as if they're struggling depending on the day, the task, their mood, or a zillion other factors. If you, like me, have ever found yourself sighing deeply and staring at the blinking cursor on your currently blank document of a draft, this book is for you. This book is also for those who have ever found themselves neck-deep in the frustration and funk of (not) writing.

The purpose of this text is to describe evidence on how smart and otherwise fairly normal people sometimes lose their minds when it comes to writing, and then show the reader how to stop being one of those people. It should be noted that this isn't a typical book about writing. From books that teach how to write to those that teach when and what to write, there are several texts on the market to help academics become better writers. This book differs in that it acknowledges and explores how emotionally and mentally challenging it can be to be a "good writer." *Why Aren't You Writing* serves as a primer for academic writers—from graduate students

---

[1] Well played, universe. Well played.

to post-docs and professors—to understand and normalize the psycho-logical, social, emotional, motivational, and physiological hurdles that can get in the way of writing productivity. It also provides strategies—some concrete and practical and others light-hearted—to engage beginning and struggling academic writers in building a healthier relationship with writing and ultimately to write more with less pain.

Organization of the Book

Successful academic writing requires not only skill but real—sometimes all too real—psychological and emotional work. After all, to become excellent and productive in our writing, we must first understand ourselves as writers—the good, the bad, and well, sometimes the quite ugly. From the inner shenanigans, such as anxiety and the imposter phenomenon, to the contextual shenanigans, such as what we write, the feedback we receive on drafts, who we write alongside, and how we work with collaborators, the chapters within this book dig into many of the stumbling blocks in the way of making progress in our academic writing. In Chapter 2, we learn how feelings of fraudulence and inadequacy—despite evidence to the contrary—can lead to writing sabotage. We will unpack our academic and writing identities as a first step toward recognizing and managing our potential cognitive distortions. Chapter 3 provides empirical evidence underlying the many shades of fear, stress, and anxiety that can plague our writing. We'll learn how paralyzing feelings of being overwhelmed can seize up any hopes we have of making progress and how to recognize when we might be under attack by our own brains. We'll also learn strategies for finding healthy engagement and flow in our writing. In Chapter 4, we explore the magical power you possess when you believe that you are a capable writer. You'll also find strategies to gain more of that magic for your own writing. Chapter 5 shows how maladaptive perfectionism can lead us to strive for unattainable writing ideals and can ultimately lead to destructive thoughts and behaviors, but research illustrates constructive ways for us to approach our writing and ourselves as writers. You'll find techniques to conquer your inner perfectionist dragon. Chapter 6 describes how we are much happier and productive writers when we have a bit of control over or interest in what, how, and when we write and work. We will delve into tricks for getting interested in our academic writing when we're not actually all that interested as well as effective strategies for finding autonomy in this bossy world. In Chapter 7, we learn about the reasons why we might block feedback on our writing. After all, feedback is effective only if we are open to receiving it. We will explore strategies for guiding others on how to give us meaningful feedback and find ways to be more open-minded about the feedback we receive about our writing. Chapter 8 discusses how writing can be a lonely endeavor and the ways in which loneliness can compromise our health and productivity. We will uncover some of the reasons why you might feel isolated in your writing and discuss strategies to help you build your writing village. Chapter 9 shows how practicing self-compassion and self-care are the secret weapons to (more) peaceful progress in your writing. We wrap up the book in an un-ending of sorts in the afterword.

Organization of Each Chapter

Each chapter begins with a discussion of evidence from research related to the many shenanigans we might experience as academic writers. Across this literature, a few themes will be evident throughout the book. First, research on academic writers is not limited to discipline or place. The samples in the studies included throughout come from psychology, education, medical fields, law, and others from all over the world. Next, because inner and contextual shenanigans are complex and often interlinked so too is the literature. As such, some ideas and strategies will appear in multiple chapters. Finally, from literature across psychology, sociology, and higher education, the research included in this book makes it quite clear that there is no quick fix to make writing easy and painless every time. Difficult and complex challenges such as writing and publishing in academia are not solved easily. For each chapter, the main points to glean from the literature are summarized in the TL;DR (too long; didn't read) section.

To help you move beyond the writing challenges holding you back, each chapter also provides practical strategies and resources for managing the shenanigans in your writing world. Such an undertaking can be a painful journey. It can be tough to think about difficult and personal topics. This book balances the hard work required for change with a bit of levity often necessary for withstanding sustained thinking and changing. It's probably here where I should mention that this isn't a typical textbook because, well, typical textbooks are borrrrring.[2] Throughout this book, you'll notice that like a river,

---

[2] *Half-heartedly apologizes to editor and publisher*

my ridiculousness runs wide and it runs deep.[3] Beyond the potential overuse of made-up words and bizarre examples, I've included actual shenanigans in the form of mildly absurd quizzes and additional activities in each chapter to provide you with a bit of comic relief oft-needed in times of writer duress-distress. You'll also find more footnotes than you perhaps expected. It turns out that I really really like footnotes.[4]

How to Use This Book

Use this book in the way it works for you, whether it's by opening it up and dropping into a chapter that sounds particularly relevant, or reading it straight through, or reflecting on a section of the research, or trying one strategy at a time. The chapters and strategies do not necessarily build upon each other so feel free to skip around, but commit to practicing at least one to two strategies to get the most benefit from each chapter. You might find it particularly helpful to read this book with others either as part of a course or study group, as discussions help normalize angsty feels and it can be helpful to hear how others manage those feels.

A Couple of Notes Before You Begin

Before you dig into this book, there's one word that I want you to think about and keep in mind as you read: *grace*. By grace, I mean taking off that ill-fitting critic's hat for both you and your writing. By grace, I mean meeting yourself where you actually are as a writer and academic—*without judgment*—and making space for yourself to grow. Spinny feelings and emotions often arise when we take a deep look at ourselves and the things that are important to us. However, there's room for all of your feels and grace to coexist—if you make room for them. Both you and your writing need and deserve grace so I challenge you to scooch on over and make some room.

Also, it's important to note that I've learned (and relearned, and then, sometimes relearned again) the lessons and strategies throughout this book. The truth is, being a peaceful and productive writer is a lot like sweeping

---

[3] Turns out I'm weird. Fa la la.
[4] Second only to my affinity for strange metaphors. My apologies in advance for freely mixing several throughout.

the floor. You don't just sweep it once and think to yourself, "Grand, now I'll never have to sweep it again. My work here is done." Humans and animals run in and around tracking mud and whatnot, our attempts at cooking leave their mark, etc. etc. Mind work is rather similar, unfortunately. Don't be discouraged if you find yourself in the funk of writing and needing to reread chapters of this book. Take heart, sweep the floor, and get back in your writing chair.

Finally, don't be discouraged or feel different if you find that your personal struggles with writing are not covered in this book. In no way do these chapters cover all of the ways that academic writing can get us down. I'd love to hear your suggestions and recommendations on what could be added to the book. Please feel free to reach out by email at szumbrunn@gmail.com.

Activity: Put Your Grace Goggles On!

Within the grace goggles lenses below, write one statement that will help you remember the grace you need and deserve on your journey to becoming a more peaceful academic writer. Skip to the perforated pages at the end of the book to cut out the grace goggles and keep them in sight while you write.

Credit Line: iStockphoto.com/adekvat

Imposter Syndrome and Writer Identity

Ah, the impostor syndrome!? The beauty of the impostor syndrome is you vacillate between extreme egomania, and a complete feeling of: "I'm a fraud! Oh god, they're on to me! I'm a fraud!"'

—**Tina Fey**

Understanding the Psychology

Fraud. That's kind of a serious idea. A quick Google image search of the word turns up images of danger signs and creepy burglars—things that most sensible humans would really rather not have associated with their names. If Tina Fey, in all her amazingness, can feel like a fraud, then so too can the rest of us. Indeed, many academic writers sometimes feel like double-dealing tricksters themselves, wondering, *"Who am I to write what I'm writing about?"* We're talking about smart people who are not, in fact, lying, cheating, snake-oil-hustling charlatans.[1] The imposter phenomenon is often associated with feelings of intellectual and professional incapability in spite of evidence to the contrary. People suffering from imposter syndrome tend to be high achievers who are exceedingly self-critical and perfectionistic, discount their ability and success, engage in self-handicapping behaviors, and fear that their perceived fraudulence or their "true" lesser selves will be discovered at any moment (Clance, 1985; Cowman & Ferrari, 2002). So, where do these beliefs come from?

---

[1] At least most of the time.

Academia: The Perfect Ecosystem for an Imposter Syndrome Epidemic

Epidemics—rapid outbreaks of infectious diseases. Think, smallpox, bird flu, selfies of food, crocs, memes, and hashtags. Could imposter syndrome be considered an epidemic? Well, not really. But its occurrence is more common than we might think in academia. Empirical findings over the last several decades estimate that over half of both men and womxn will experience at least one episode of the imposter phenomenon in their lives (Matthews & Clance, 1985; Vaughn et al., 2019).

When are we most likely to come down with a nasty case of imposter syndrome? Similar to other epidemics, imposter syndrome can strike when the conditions are right. And, unfortunately, academia presents the perfect ecosystem for widespread feelings of imposterism in its inhabitants, especially when it comes to writing. There are three primary conditions that incubate imposter syndrome experiences: during a new experience, while receiving an evaluation, and during an unexpected experience (Fujie, 2010). As you can tell from the meticulously illustrated Figure 2.1, these conditions often apply to the writing habitats of graduate students and newly minted academics.

First, let's consider some of the new experiences you might face as a graduate student or new academic. The first, obviously, is graduate school or your new position. It's new. And exciting.[2] But sometimes new and exciting situations can be a little scary, too, no? Humans prefer predictability (Miller, 1981). It's comforting to know what's around the corner or what we might expect next. Unfortunately, such predictability is not necessarily common in new situations.

Figure 2.1 Ecosystem Considerations

	New Experience?	Receive Evaluation?	Unexpected Experience?
Graduate Student	x	x	x
Newly Minted Academic	x	x	x

---

[2] Consider how long you dreamed of your very own brass nameplate with the letters "PhD" on it.

In this new space, the type of writing you're asked to do may also be new. Take the dissertation, for example. Completing my dissertation was one of the most difficult things I have ever done. In fact, I regularly referred to the project as "Dark Looming Cloud" and housed all materials for the project in a three-inch binder illustrated with several actual dark, looming clouds. And now that I'm done, I know I'll kill it the next time I do another dissertation. Regrettably, by its very nature the dissertation is a new genre that students typically need only—and often painfully—to complete once. New genres, however, are ones that academics find themselves faced with time and time again. From research proposals to grant applications, academics frequently find opportunities for repeated practice, which can lead to higher beliefs of efficacy (see Chapter 4 [Writing Self-efficacy] for more on this). Nonetheless, there's a first time for everything, and that first time can feel 50 shades of terrifying (for a detailed discussion of all things scary, see the next chapter [Writing Stress and Anxiety]).

Next, we turn to evaluations. So. Many. Evaluations. From high-stakes tests to the dissertation, and from annual performance evaluations to publication and tenure review, it can feel like every task is an examination ritual and all our efforts are under the microscope. Then, sometimes anticipating the feedback that we will receive on our recently submitted work can feel equally overwhelming. *Will it be good enough? Will that metaphor I used about epidemics resonate? Did I use the word "although" too many times? Should I have used a different theoretical framework?* Cut to the potential emotional fallout associated with receiving critical feedback. Certainly, receiving feedback on our efforts can provide valuable information about our learning and writing progress, but such feedback can also knock us down. And when we are nursing our bruised egos, it can sometimes feel like we need to push those feelings down and feel proud of our work—that of which we might not actually feel terribly proud.

Amidst the new experiences and years of evaluation, it likely comes as no surprise that our feelings of inadequacy can be heightened when we stumble into unexpected experiences. When you signed up for this position, you might have thought that being surrounded by bright people sounded amazing. Thinking and reading, then talking and writing about your thinking and reading . . . ah, academia. Throw in a glittery unicorn, some fluffy clouds, and a batch of freshly baked chocolate chip cookies and it might just be a vision of heaven. In the swirly dreaminess of your fantasy (and often, or at least sometimes, the reality) of academia, you might not have considered that such surroundings might be somewhat intimidating. I mean, as intellectuals, we are typically excited when we get opportunities to push our thinking, but there is a limit when such excitement becomes overwhelming. For example, when we dive into a new research interest, we might begin in a state of inspired exhilaration, but then the inundation of unfamiliar literature and potentially (un?)welcome feedback can turn our state of enthusiasm into one of panic. And, with so many smart people doing lots of important things around every corner, it can be easy to measure ourselves and our writing against others and not feel good enough.

Wondering what might be worse than the combination of all of these experiences? Throw them together in a big ol' black box of no one talking about it and *voila*! We might then find ourselves a mess of feelings and unhealthy coping strategies. In one study, Hutchins and Rainbolt (2017) found that some faculty reported efforts to lessen the stress associated with their imposter feelings by working more or through alcohol or other substance abuse. Unfortunately, engaging in avoidant coping responses such as these provided faculty with only temporary relief and put them at a greater risk of burnout or depression. Data also suggest that the persistence of elevated feelings of imposterism over time—especially when kept private—can be emotionally exhausting (Hutchins, 2015). On the other hand, engaging in coping techniques such as actively seeking feedback and support can productively address the core issues of imposter concerns (Hutchins & Rainbolt, 2017).

Who Is Most at Risk for Feeling "Impostery"?

The imposter phenomenon seems to be more common among people with advanced degrees, high achievers, those in the creative fields, and people who work in highly competitive and stressful work conditions[3] (Hutchins, 2015). Especially susceptible are those who feel less secure in their positions such as graduate students and untenured faculty, both seemingly in professional purgatory.

Though findings are mixed in the literature, there is some evidence to suggest that individuals with feminine and undifferentiated gender-role

---

[3] Sound familiar, academic homies?

orientation might wrestle more with imposter demons (Patzak et al., 2017). Indeed, the term "imposter syndrome" was coined by Pauline Rose Clance and Suzanne Imes in a 1970s study of highly successful womxn who felt like frauds despite their achievements (Clance & Imes, 1978). In a recent international survey of womxn in higher education, Vaughn et al. (2019) found that 95% of female scholars show at least moderate levels of the imposter phenomenon, and two-thirds of them experience frequent or intense levels. Moreover, their findings and the findings from others suggest that imposterism is just as likely to affect womxn regardless of their academic position, status, seniority, or type of institution (Dua, 2007). People who exemplify sociocultural characteristics counter to the norm of the institution, such as people of color and first-generation students may also have disproportionately more imposter fears than their peers (Gardner & Holley, 2011; Posselt, 2018).

Writer Identity Deficit Disorder

Writer identity deficit disorder (WIDD) is a fairly common disorder characterized by misguided, yet concrete, idolized perceptions associated with the words "writer" or "author." These visions can vary from rich and famous individuals wearing dark-rimmed glasses and blazers, carrying books and fancy recycled notebooks, to wizards who turn caffeine into words. Actually, WIDD is a completely fictitious disorder that I just made up. However, evidence does suggest that when we hold grandiose beliefs about who writers are and what writers do, then it's much more difficult to self-identify as "real" authors ourselves (Walsh, 2018). As a matter of fact, the word "author" has roots in Middle English and Old French relating to invention, origination, and influence (Author, n.d.) and such associations might seem daunting to those who don't feel particularly inventive, original, or influential. When our subconscious beliefs about writing and ourselves as writers are inferior or destructive, the ways we approach writing can be maladaptive and the quality of our writing suffers as well (White & Bruning, 2005). In short, perceptions matter. What we think affects what we see, and what we see affects what we do.

The Power of Perceptions

As humans, we are rocking an absurdly influential organ in our bodies—the brain. Because of our brains, we are able to balance and talk

Evidence Checklist: Writing Imposterness

You may be suffering from writing imposterness if you:

- [ ] Second guess your writing by hemming and hawing* over every word, sentence, punctuation mark, etc.

- [ ] Procrastinate by finding REALLY important things to do other than write (e.g., *"Who could write in this mess?!"*)

- [ ] Avoid the end by over-researching (e.g., *"There have to be sources that I'm missing!"*) to delay submitting and receiving judgment (and being unmasked)

- [ ] Partially commit to the writing you submit (e.g., *"Of course I got that feedback, I wasn't really trying."*)

---

* How does one actually "haw," anyway?

and feel, we can make snap decisions about our new colleagues or what to do when we see a massive bear in the distance, and we can put our thoughts on the page to convey mostly coherent ideas. The brain can be duplicitous, as well. Some studies suggest that our brains can be tricked into believing untruths, including things that never happened (Loftus, 2005).[4] As psychologist Elizabeth Loftus (2003) wrote, "People's memories are not only the sum of all that they have done, but there is more to them: The memories are also the sum of what they have thought, what they have been told, what we believe" (p. 872). Unfortunately, some of our memories are derived from what we tell ourselves about ourselves. When it comes to our writing (and life in general), it's in our best interest to learn to use this crazy power for good by dropkicking the "meanie-self" and giving a hug to the kinder, gentler "loving-self."

---

[4] Like being abducted by aliens . . . horrifying (McNally, 2003), or past-life experiences as a Viking, Druid priestess, the Pharaoh's scribe, or a polar bear (Meyersburg et al., 2009).

Reality Check

I know. The struggle to feel worthy is real. The truth is, however, you wouldn't be here fighting this dragon if you weren't ready for it. You're here. Whether you earned it or you tricked everyone—you're here. When the not-so-fraudster Tina Fey finds herself agonizing in a personal "anxious, stunted brain cloud," she takes a step back (2011, p. 274). When you're in your own brain cloud feeling like a fraud, pause and think about who and what you see around you in your school/work environment. Bright and shiny successful writers? People making writing look super easy? Now factor in the impressions you've taken away from social network sites such as Facebook or Instagram. You know, the perceptions people hope others take away when they post "proof" of their happy and amazing existence (whether or not the evidence is independent of reality). Our impressions of others can impact the ways in which we perceive the brightness and shininess of our own lives and success (de Vries & Kühne, 2015). Unfortunately, writing, learning, and success are not always bright and shiny[5] or easy to come by, but we live in a culture that equates smart with easy. We often therefore go to great lengths to hide just how hard we work for it. Instances such as the "Stanford Duck Syndrome," which describes the tendency to project the appearance of calm and cool while paddling madly below the surface, and the "Penn Face," which describes the false impression of seeming collected and in control suggest that hiding effort might be particularly prevalent on academic campuses (Scelfo, 2015). Seeing others for who they really are can help us liberate a more positive view of ourselves.

Additionally, there is a sense of calm that can wash over us when we are not only realistic about what we do well but also when we are clear about what we're working on to improve. This sense of relief is related to honesty—owning who we are today. Getting to this place takes courage, and mustering courage can be exhausting, as courage entails actively pursuing your fears. And, if you're afraid of it, it probably means that it—or some aspect of it—is important to you. So it's worth it.

---

[5] Unless, of course, you count the actual sweat you produce while working as "shiny."

TL;DR Summary

- Sometimes we can feel like frauds, like our true identities as ninnies who don't belong in academia will be discovered. When there's evidence that we actually do belong, this experience is known as the imposter phenomenon.

- Unfortunately, the imposter phenomenon is very common, especially in academia.

- Three primary conditions breed imposter tendencies: new experiences, receiving an evaluation, and during unexpected experiences. These conditions are lurking around every corner of higher education.

- Those with advanced degrees, high achievers, individuals in creative fields, and people who work in highly competitive and stressful work conditions (a.k.a. higher ed) are susceptible to feeling like imposters. Especially vulnerable are those who feel less secure in their positions, such as graduate students or untenured faculty members. Those with feminine and undifferentiated gender-role orientation and those who exemplify sociocultural characteristics counter to the norm are at even greater risk for developing imposter fears.

- It's difficult to self-identify as a writer when we hold unrealistic beliefs about who writers are and what they do. Perceptions matter—be mindful of your thoughts.

Essential Strategies for Productive (and Sane) Writing

If/when you feel like an imposter in your writing, there are things to keep in mind and strategies that can help you slay the imposter dragon and begin to feel the sense of belonging you deserve. Choose one to two ideas from the following sections to get started.

The Fast Track to Expertville

Just kidding. Sorry if you thought I was serious. Similar to the disappointing absence of magical ways of getting rich or successful overnight, suddenly becoming an expert writer (or dancer or chef or zookeeper) is unrealistic. Several decades of research suggest that the road to Expertville is quite long . . . like 10,000 hours long (Ericsson et al., 1993). No, seriously. Expertise requires roughly two decades of focused practice (Kellogg & Whiteford, 2009). It's also important to keep the law of practice in mind, whereby we often see greater gains in improvement from early and middle stages of practice (Newell & Rosenbloom, 1981). Unfortunately, this means that evidence of our writing progress is more difficult to see when we're, say, in or beyond our 19th year of school. Also remember that successfully completing more complex tasks generally follow practice and development (i.e., say farewell to the days of high school English class theme essays and hello to years of grant proposals and journal articles).

Keep a Failure CV

"What is a failure CV and why would I ever want one of those?" you may ask. Whereas your actual CV highlights the successes of your career, your failure CV features your career disappointments, disasters, rejections, and catastrophes. Importantly, your failure CV also describes the lessons you've learned from your professional fiascos. For example, my own personal failure CV includes changing my undergrad major three times (decisions are hard), my first experiment that got null results (research is hard), and the five (!) journals that turned down one of my manuscripts before it got published (revisions are hard). The silver lining? Through these difficult setbacks, I've learned to trust my gut more, that research is messy—especially meaningful research—and that dogged determination can pay off (for more on productive responses to failure, see Chapter 4 [Writing Self-efficacy]). Keeping a CV of my flops has given me the opportunity to reflect and gain perspective. It's helped me see the steps that have led me to success, and seeing others' failure CVs has helped me see that I'm not alone in my struggles. Failure is not only normal—it's necessary. Let's stop pretending it doesn't exist.

Have a Heart . . . for Yourself

As cheesy as it might sound, I believe that we live our best lives—and write our best writing—when we are our most authentic selves. Unfortunately, it's impossible to be our authentic selves if we don't think very highly of the "self" in question. What does that authenticity look like? For starters, it means being honest with yourself and being OK with the world seeing the honest you, and this requires self-compassion (for an extended discussion on self-compassion, see Chapter 9 [The Importance of Wellness and Self-Care]). Research suggests links between self-compassion and the imposter phenomenon. In one study, Patzak et al., (2017) found that students who were more self-compassionate were more resistant to feelings of imposterism than their peers with lower levels of self-compassion.

One way to show your writer-self a little love is to be mindful of the way that you talk to yourself. Which talk are you buying into? You get to choose: you can either buy into positive thoughts or negative self-talk. For instance, if you continuously tell yourself that you're an imposter then it's likely that you're going to keep feeling that way. Instead, think about why you *might actually* belong. Maybe you're not an expert yet, sure, but who *really* is? Everyone has something to learn. Think about the reasons around why it's good to be you. What do you add to the place you learn/work? When it comes to writing, what do you do particularly well? Make an actual list and focus on that when you start feeling a bit impostery.

Build Your Village

Hours (read: years) of statistics training reminds us that not everyone can be an outlier, but everyone can *feel* like an outlier, at least sometimes. To help counter imposter beliefs, it's a good idea to find and lean on your village. Who are the people in your village? First, consider your colleagues or friends who might share similar experiences and thought patterns. Seeing and hearing that others feel the way we do can be comforting because it makes us recognize that we're not alone (much more on this in Chapter 8 [Finding Social Support for Writing]).

Next, who is presently or could be your mentor? Maybe your adviser or supervisor? A colleague? These are the people who support you and can guide you in a positive direction. I'm a firm believer that you can never have too many encouraging mentors, especially in academic ecosystems.

Finally, consider inviting a counselor or therapist to your village. For many, individual therapy can be particularly helpful. Leaning on professionals to give you specific tools to break free of your imposter beliefs is smart, not weak (#TherapyIsDope).

NEXT STEPS ────────────────────────────────

☐ Note to Self: Research shows that it takes 10,000 hours (!) to become an expert. There are no shortcuts to becoming an expert writer.

- Draft a "Failure CV" that details your career missteps and the important lessons you've learned from the struggles that have helped make you into the writer and scholar that you are today.

- Make a list of the things you're decent at when it comes to writing. Then put that list in a place where you'll see again.

- Define who is in your village—who is it that supports, encourages, and empowers you? Then have a conversation about your impostery feelings with the members of your village and dig into the fairness of those feelings.

EXTRA RESOURCES

Roche, J. M. (2013). *The empress has no clothes: Conquering self-doubt to embrace success.* Berrett-Koehler Publishers.

Young, V. (2011). *The secret thoughts of successful women: Why capable people suffer from the impostor syndrome and how to thrive in spite of it.* Crown Publishing Group.

HUMOR BREAK

Quiz: Which Emoji Is Your Imposter Syndrome?[6]

Complete the following quiz to reveal your level of imposterness.

1. Pick a smiley: a.   b.   c.

2. Pick a symbol: a.   b.   c.

3. Pick a figure of anatomy: a. b. c. ᎒᎒

4. Pick an object: a. b. c.

---

[6] Disclaimer: This quiz is ridiculous and in no way scientifically accurate.

MOSTLY A's: Low Imposterness: Like the flamenco dancer, you feel comfortable in your skin and aren't afraid to strut your stuff (that dress, though!). In addition to the dance floor, you own most, if not all of your success. You believe in your ability and feel pride and satisfaction when things go well.

MOSTLY B's: Moderate Imposterness: Although you worry sometimes that your success might simply be due to luck or an error, or that people might discover that you don't belong, other times you're able to ride the waves of your earned success.

MOSTLY C's: High Imposterness: Warning. Warning. Warning. Imposter feelings alert. Much akin to an invasion of body snatchers, you often experience uncomfortable feelings of phoniness. You catch yourself worried that people will find out you don't belong in a community of intellectuals and scholarly writers.

Activity: "I Belong Here" Contract

This is an agreement made by A Recovering Writing Imposter Who Definitely Belongs, _____ (hereafter referred to as The Belonger).

1. **First Guess Promise**. Saving indecisiveness for important decisions at the bakery counter,[7] The Belonger will stop second-guessing writing decisions big and small and make more assured choices while writing. The Belonger will realize simply resting on a word, sentence, or punctuation mark is just that—a rest, or a "for now"—and that the decision can be changed in the next draft.[8]

2. **Task Attacking**. The Belonger will no longer put off writing by procrastinating.[9] Instead, The Belonger will attack writing tasks. After all, Belongers know that they have important-ish things to share with the world. When times are tough, The Belonger will only rely on distractivating tasks (Distractivated, n.d.), or tasks that

---

[7] Sour cream–and–blueberry muffin? Warm and gooey cinnamon roll? Goat cheese–and–chive biscuit? How does anyone decide?!

[8] . . . because there's ALWAYS another draft.

[9] You know, like procrastibaking, procrasticleaning, or procrastiplanningforclass.

distract the writer in such a way that activates creative writing ideas and motivation. For example, you might consider listening to an interesting but completely unrelated podcast through the lens of your writing project (writing/drawing notes during this time is essential).

3. **Just Do It**. Writing: *This is the process that never ends, yes it goes on and on, my friend . . .* The Belonger will realize when this super annoying (and unproductive) tune is playing on repeat.[10] And promptly turn it off. The Belonger will recognize that one more source is about as valuable as your wisdom teeth. The Belonger will also realize that the idea of "perfect" is a cruel joke created by misery fairies (check out Chapter 5 for a detailed discussion of maladaptive perfectionism) and will just submit the draft already.

4. **#LikeABoss**. The Belonger will own the work submitted. The Belonger will proceed to walk past a mirror and point to the reflection from the side without really looking to show the world vacant room who's the boss. The Belonger will also realize that any feedback received does not define the writer, but rather the direction of the writing (visit Chapter 7 [Embracing the Feedback Process] for a potential attitude adjustment around feedback).

5. *Signed:* _____

(The Belonger)

References

Author. (n.d.). *OxfordDictionaries.com*. https://en.oxforddictionaries.com/definition/author.

Clance, P. R. (1985). *The impostor phenomenon: Overcoming the fear that haunts your success*. Peachtree Pub Ltd.

Clance, P. R., & Imes, S. A. (1978). The imposter phenomenon in high achieving women: Dynamics and therapeutic intervention. *Psychotherapy: Theory, Research & Practice, 15*(3), 241–247. doi:10.1037/h0086006

Cowman, S. E., & Ferrari, J. R. (2002). "Am I for real?" Predicting impostor tendencies from self-handicapping and affective components. *Social Behavior and Personality: An International Journal, 30*(2), 119–125. doi:10.2224/sbp.2002.30.2.119

de Vries, D. A., & Kühne, R. (2015). Facebook and self-perception: Individual susceptibility to negative social comparison on Facebook. *Personality and Individual Differences, 86*, 217–221. doi:10.1016/j.paid.2015.05.029

---

[10] Just make it stop.

Distractivated. (n.d.). *Urban dictionary*. https://www.urbandictionary.com/define.php?term=Distractivated.

Dua, P. (2007). Feminist mentoring and female graduate student success: Challenging gender inequality in higher education. *Sociology Compass, 1*(2), 594–612. doi:10.1111/j.1751-9020.2007.00042.x

Ericsson, K. A., Krampe, R. T., & Tesch-Römer, C. (1993). The role of deliberate practice in the acquisition of expert performance. *Psychological Review, 100*(3), 363–406. doi:10.1037/0033-295X.100.3.363

Fey, T. (2011). *Bossypants*. Hachette UK.

Fujie, R. (2010). Development of the State Impostor Phenomenon Scale. *Japanese Psychological Research, 52*(1), 1–11. doi:10.1111/j.1468-5884.2009.00417.x

Gardner, S. K., & Holley, K. A. (2011). "Those invisible barriers are real": The progression of first-generation students through doctoral education. *Equity & Excellence in Education, 44*(1), 77–92. doi:10.1080/10665684.2011.529791

Hutchins, H. M. (2015). Outing the imposter: A study exploring imposter phenomenon among higher education faculty. *New Horizons in Adult Education and Human Resource Development, 27*(2), 3–12. doi:10.1002/nha3.20098

Hutchins, H. M., & Rainbolt, H. (2017). What triggers imposter phenomenon among academic faculty? A critical incident study exploring antecedents, coping, and development opportunities. *Human Resource Development International, 20*(3), 194–214. doi:10.1080/13678868.2016.1248205

Kellogg, R. T., & Whiteford, A. P. (2009). Training advanced writing skills: The case for deliberate practice. *Educational Psychologist, 44*(4), 250–266. doi:10.1080/00461520903213600

Loftus, E. F. (2003). Make-believe memories. *American Psychologist, 58*(11), 867–873. doi:10.1037/0003-066X.58.11.867

Loftus, E. F. (2005). Planting misinformation in the human mind: A 30-year investigation of the malleability of memory. *Learning & Memory, 12*(4), 361–366. doi:10.1101/lm.94705

Matthews, G., & Clance, P. R. (1985). Treatment of the impostor phenomenon in psychotherapy clients. *Psychotherapy in Private Practice, 3*(1), 71–81.

McNally, R. J. (2003). Recovering memories of trauma: A view from the laboratory. *Current Directions in Psychological Science, 12*(1), 32–35.

Meyersburg, C. A., Bogdan, R., Gallo, D. A., & McNally, R. J. (2009). False memory propensity in people reporting recovered memories of past lives. *Journal of Abnormal Psychology, 118*(2), 399–404. doi:10.1037/a0015371

Miller, S. M. (1981). Predictability and human stress: Toward a clarification of evidence and theory. *Advances in Experimental Social Psychology, 14*, 203–256.

Newell, A., & Rosenbloom, P. S. (1981). *Mechanisms of skill acquisition and the law of practice.* In J. R. Anderson (Ed.), *Cognitive skills and their acquisition* (pp. 1–55). Lawrence Erlbaum Associates, Inc.

Patzak, A., Kollmayer, M., & Schober, B. (2017). Buffering impostor feelings with kindness: The mediating role of self-compassion between gender-role orientation and the impostor phenomenon. *Frontiers in Psychology, 8,* Article 1289. doi:10.3389/fpsyg.2017.01289

Posselt, J. R. (2018). Rigor and support in racialized learning environments: The case of graduate education. *New Directions for Higher Education, 2018*(181), 59–70. doi:10.1002/he.20271

Scelfo, J. (2015, July 27). Suicide on campus and the pressure of perfection. *The New York Times.* http://www.nytimes.com

Vaughn, A. R., Taasoobshirazi, G., & Johnson, M. L. (2019). Impostor phenomenon and motivation: Womxn in higher education. *Studies in Higher Education.* doi:10.1080/03075079.2019.1568976

Walsh, M. (2018). *Examining students' writer identity in the transition from high school to college: A mixed methods study* [Unpublished doctoral dissertation]. Virginia Commonwealth University.

White, M. J., & Bruning, R. (2005). Implicit writing beliefs and their relation to writing quality. *Contemporary Educational Psychology, 30*(2), 166–189. doi:10.1016/j.cedpsych.2004.07.002

Writing Stress and Anxiety

"Beware the Jabberwock, my son! The jaws that bite, the claws that catch!
Beware the Jubjub bird, and shun the frumious Bandersnatch!"
>   **—Lewis Carroll, "Jabberwocky"**

Understanding the Psychology

With jaws that bite and claws that catch, we can all agree that monsters—
even ones with charming names like the Jubjub bird—are scary
(and *frumious*, obviously). And sometimes, writing might seem like a
monster—an intimidating beast surely out to get you. In fact, Wellington
(2010) found that many graduate students used words like *fear, stress,* and
isolation to describe their experiences with writing. The American Psychological Association [n.d.] characterizes anxiety as feelings of tension,
worried thoughts, and physical changes like increased blood pressure.
Unfortunately, anxiety and its sister, depression, are all too common
for academics. According to a recent study, nearly 37% of academics
suffer from mental health problems (Guthrie et al., 2018). Like you read
about in the last chapter, academia is the perfect incubator for breeding
emotional distress. And the seeds of distress might start germinating
when students are in graduate school. In a large study of economics PhD
programs in the United States, researchers found that 18% of students
experienced moderate to severe symptoms of anxiety and/or depression,
which is nearly three times the national average (Barreira et al., 2018). It's
not surprising that students near the end of their programs were much
more likely than those first beginning their adventures in PhD-Land to
report severe symptoms. After all, many programs end with a special form
of torture: the master's thesis or the doctoral dissertation. Then there's
a bonus for the ladies, because research suggests higher rates of writing

anxiety for womxn (Huerta et al., 2017). And, as if this plague of anxiety wasn't enough on its own, findings from several studies show that those tormented by writing anxiety are often also afflicted with a writer's block (Boice & Johnson, 1984; Boice, 1997), produce poorer written products (Onwuegbuzie, 1999), have lower grades (Martinez et al., 2011), lack confidence, and have unrealistic expectations of what comprises good writing (Wachholz & Etheridge, 1996). What is it that can make the wild thing of writing just so terrifying? Lots of things, actually, but it's important to recognize what distinguishes fear from anxiety.

Deconstructing Fear and Anxiety

Similar to fear, anxiety acts as a biological warning system that prepares us to fight, flee, or freeze in dangerous situations. Potentially dangerous situations might include the shark that could be lurking under the dark water where you're swimming, your grandma's collection of dolls (just no), and, er, writing. The biological warnings of both fear and anxiety can include a host of uncomfortable experiences, from increased heart rate and blood pressure to sweating, shortness of breath, and a need to use the restroom (#Awkward). Indeed, the mere thought of my grandma's creepy dolls with eyes that blink on their own (!) make my hands feel clammy.

Although our bodies react to fear and anxiety in similar ways, I want to point out a subtle, yet important, difference between the two. Fear is evolution's gift to us, warning us of immediate harm (e.g., a baseball hurtling at your face). Anxiety, on the other hand, requires your imagination. In her blog, author Sharon Salzberg (2019, February 7) describes anxiety as "free-floating hyperactivity of the mind." I think this summarizes it perfectly. In a way, writing anxiety is self-generated fear. The control-value theory of achievement emotions (Pekrun, 2006) suggests we experience fear when (1) we value the task, but we also (2) feel as if succeeding on it is out of our control, often because we don't believe in our capabilities to meet task demands (for more on our ability beliefs, see Chapter 4 [Writing Self-efficacy]). Getting stuck while writing can lead some to imagine twisty, negative thoughts about what this stuckness might mean about their writing or their future as a writer or scholar. And for some of us, our imaginations really outdo themselves. Noticing when your imagination is on a destructive roll can help you recognize when you are under attack by your own brain.

Paralyzing Overwhelmedness[1]

Everywhere you turn these days, no matter whom you ask, people say how busy they are. For most, likely it is not an exaggeration. As an example, let's take a look-see at your calendar. What do you notice? My guess is quite a lot. Next, let's turn to your list of scholarly/writing projects and the number of goals that you have for each of those projects. That shish is overwhelming even before you pile on the other responsibilities of your life. You are definitely busy. But each time we mention how busy we are, our brains hear us and we reinforce our feelings of overwhelmedness. From there, things can get straight spinny.

There are approximately one zillion[2] things that can make writing seem overwhelming. For starters, as academic writers, we are typically writing for someone or something, which means that there is ample opportunity to be judged. Thinking about being judged is not always the most comfortable. The peer review process literally requires someone to judge our writing. Coupling angst about upcoming judgment with high stakes can lead to some other fairly chilling thoughts. What if the draft isn't good? What if it's terrible or they hate it? What does that mean for me? About me? Does that mean I'm not very good? Does that mean that I don't belong here? You see the direction of this spinny line of thinking, right? These thoughts can leave us thinking that maybe even our grandma's creepy doll collection is preferable to writing.

In psychology, these spinny thoughts relate to catastrophizing,[3] or exaggerating the negative consequences of events or decisions. In other words, this is your overactive imagination at work, spiraling to get you to believe things are drastically worse than they actually are. It's easy to lose perspective when things seem downright awful, and that swamp of despair can be really hard to escape. It is in this swamp where we might find ourselves in a catatonic state, paralyzed by our too-full calendars, lists of writing projects/goals/things-to-do, and swampy despair thoughts.

When I find myself in this dark place, I tend to ruminate on those swampy despair thoughts. To ruminate literally means to "chew over" and cows might come to mind.[4] When cows are chowing down on some

---

[1] Like Lewis Carroll, I make up words when I don't like those available to me.

[2] I've also been informed that one zillion is not a real number. Whatever.

[3] I promise that catastrophizing is a real word, coined by psychologist Albert Ellis (Ellis, 1962).

[4] Sometimes cows randomly come to my mind because I'm from Nebraska. Weird? Maybe. This, however, is not a random cow association.

delicious grass, they chew it, then swallow, regurgitate, and chew it up again. In a similar-but-not-quite-as-gross way, when we ruminate, we chew on our worrying thoughts again and again in our minds. Playing this fretty chatter on repeat can take a toll on our brains and our bodies (Nolen-Hoeksema et al., 2008). However, there are actions we can take to stop chewing over our negative writing thoughts—even before they begin. Bringing awareness to your ruminating thoughts and identifying them as harmful is the first step. Then, remind yourself that you are in charge of your brain and take control of your thoughts. Plan ahead and think of a positive thought, maybe an optimistic idea or a happy memory, to interrupt and redirect your next potential rumination session with your planned positive thought (Eagleson et al., 2016). Better yet, the next time you start to worry about your writing, vividly imagine a positive scenario where things work out in your favor. In one recent study when high worriers were trained to create vivid (e.g., including details related to what they saw, heard, felt, smelled, or tasted) and emotionally laden mental images related to personally worrisome topics, they experienced higher control of worry and more positive moods (Skodzik et al., 2017).

Reframing Anxiety

Although severe anxiety is often disorganizing and debilitating, moderate anxiety directs our attention and motivation[5] (Hoehn-Saric & McLeod, 1988). Indeed, challenging tasks like writing might often present moderate levels of anxiety for many academic writers. The trick is finding the sweet spot of challenge, à la Goldilocks—somewhere between too difficult and too easy. Research and theory suggest that by combining the conditions of just-manageable challenges, a clear series of goals, and the continuous processing of feedback about the progress being made can induce the mental state and experience of flow (Csikszentmihalyi, 1975, 1997). What in the actual tarnation is flow, you ask? For starters, it is the opposite of stuck. It's like finding yourself in some time warp zone that whisks you off to a miraculous universe where you lose track of time and are insanely productive. Sounds enchanting, no? It kind of is. Studies show that when writers and other creatives are in flow, they are in a state of deep concentration, control, and calm; experience the activity as intrinsically

---

[5] Hello, deadlines. We see you.

Box 3.1 Evidence Checklist: Conditions Necessary for Finding Flow in Your Writing

☐ Set clear, proximal, and measurable goals for your writing task.

☐ Double-check that each of your goals for your allotted writing time today are indeed clear (i.e., a stranger would be able to pick up your goal list and get to work—seriously, *that* clear).

☐ Double-check that each of your goals is actually realistic for the time you have to devote to writing during this block. Consider breaking up your writing block into small chunks (e.g., 25 minutes) and choose a super-realistic goal to tackle during each mini-block. Then evaluate how realistic you were when the timer goes off. Don't berate yourself if you under- or overestimated the time you needed to accomplish your goal. This is pretty normal and takes practice to calibrate. Readjust. Breathe. Begin again.

☐ Check the level of challenge for each of your writing goals. Ensure that each goal presents a just-manageable challenge. Understanding what "just-manageable" means for you may take some time to get right.*

☐ Keep an eye on your progress as you write. What is working and what isn't? Try to keep perspective and adjust your goals and strategies as necessary.

---

* Homegirl Goldilocks took three tries with each of her goals of sitting, eating, AND sleeping at the Three Bears' cottage.

motivating; and sense that time has passed faster than normal (Nakamura & Csikszentmihalyi, 2014; Perry, 1999). For example, one writer described his flow experience: "At the moment it is flowing it is always incredibly easy. I do not think I've ever been in a creative process where I do not feel afterwards that I have cheated. I just think it simply came, so it was amazing that I lost the feeling of time" (Chemi, 2016, p. 41). To get to the dreamy state of flow with your writing, focus on getting the conditions right with the checklist in Box 3.1.

Angsty Itchy Thoughts

Not too long ago, I had a mean run-in with a patch of poison ivy. I thought I might actually scratch my arms straight off my torso. Y'all, I could not stop scratching, and it didn't seem to matter that I knew that scratching like a wild animal would not ease the itch. Sometimes, the angsty chatter in our minds about our writing or about ourselves as scholars/writers makes it feel as though our thoughts could itch. We find ourselves in late-night overthinking sessions stealing our sleep. And wait, there's more. Let us not forget the torturous early morning and midday overthinking sessions. It would be so lovely to lather an anti-itch cream over these thoughts because they tend to put a choke hold on our progress and well-being. In the absence of a miracle cream, I would instead have an (unhealthy) angry, come-to-Jesus with myself, "Self, what's wrong with you?! Pull it together. For reals this time," as though I wasn't serious the last time I/we had this conversation.

I want to normalize the angsty, itchy thoughts in our heads or the overly critical things we sometimes say to ourselves when we don't/can't write. They are dreadful. They are also regrettably normal and *not* a sign that we are weak or broken. When I learned just how prevalent anxiety and depression are in our world—especially for academics—it came as a relief. It stopped being my problem—something that made me weird, different, or broken—and made it something fairly normal, albeit still pretty ratty. With this realization, I was able to lift the judgy glasses that I so often wore to look at myself and see my thoughts and actions with more compassion (read more about self-compassion in Chapter 9 [The Importance of Wellness and Self-Care]). For me, replacing my angry, self-come-to-Jesus with a more kind-hearted conversation helps me turn down the writing anxiety dial.

Most importantly, please remember that seeking help or finding someone to talk to is a characteristic of strength. Grad school and academia in general can be intense. Check out the resources at the end of this chapter to be proactive about your emotional health.

TL;DR Summary

- Writing (or even *thinking* about writing) can lead graduate students and other academics to feelings of anxiety and dread.

- Although fear and anxiety can physically and emotionally feel the same, anxiety needs our imagination to survive and grow. The first step to squashing writing anxiety is recognizing when your thoughts are gaining negative momentum.

- Rehearsing the contents of our calendars, scholarly projects, writing goals, and to-do lists can send us into a panic, and in that panic we might catastrophize or exaggerate and ruminate or dwell on our negative thoughts. Again, awareness of your thoughts can stop writing anxiety before—or shortly after—it begins.

- Believe it or not, there is such a thing as the "right" amount of writing anxiety. Challenge or a moderate level of stress is a necessary ingredient of achieving the mental state of flow, or the state of deep concentration, motivation, and control.

Essential Strategies for Productive (and Sane) Writing

Depending on the project, deadline, audience, or a thousand other things, writing can make us feel anxious, but there are ways to help calm the worry storm and make progress on our work one step at a time. Read the following sections and choose one or two strategies to begin.

Acknowledging and Saying Farewell to the Funk

I'm going to be real—I hate those shirts and bumper stickers boasting "POSITIVE VIBES ONLY." I see them and think to myself, *Yeah, that sounds nice—fairly unrealistic if you are me—but nice.* Similarly, in writing this chapter, I found several toxic quotes from famous authors about how they don't believe in writer's block, as if it is a luxury or a myth.[6] Writer's block

---

[6] Like Bigfoot, the 5-second rule, or learning styles (Willingham et al., 2015).

is often the manifestation of anxiety, which is most certainly real for many of us. It is unfortunate and almost offensive to pretend that it doesn't exist.

When we find ourselves in the funk, or in moments of intense emotional and physical arousal, it can be difficult to implement the cognitive control necessary to calm ourselves down. However, that's precisely what is necessary, and there's hope[7] because it can get easier with practice. There is so much power in taking a step back and making a conscious decision to stop feeding into overwhelming negative feelings. However, this cannot happen unless we first notice when we are catastrophizing. We have to notice when our imaginations and negative feelings are getting the best of us.

I also want to reiterate how critical it is to be careful about what we say to ourselves (and to others about ourselves) in these moments. Just like the word, *busy*, discussed earlier in the chapter, words and phrases such as *awful, terrible, I hate this*, or *I'm going to die*, do not reduce your Negative Nelly potential. Instead, these messages intensify your negative feelings. Replace your negative inner monologue with more productive self-talk like *this is unpleasant, but it is just a feeling*, or *I think I need to revise my writing goals for today*. Learn more about productive self-talk in Chapter 9 [The Importance of Wellness and Self-Care].

Writing Projects Have Personality: Give It a Name

I believe that each of our projects have a personality of their own. While some seem crotchety and curmudgeonly, some feel strong and empowering, and others seem light and fun. Each project's personality comes from our experience with the project—how we feel when we work on it, our role on the project, our collaborators on the work, etcetera. As such, we have relationships with our writing projects. I think it's weird to have a relationship with ~~someone~~ something without a name.[8] Names give a bit of life to your projects and help you develop relationships with them. Names also give you something to honor . . . or yell at—both of which our writing often deserves. For example, I named my dissertation "Lillian" and called her "Lilly" on good days. Lillian, her proper name, was reserved for the struggle days (kind of like the way adults use their kids' full names when they are *really* in trouble). On some days, friends would ask about

---

[7] Speaking of hope, humor can positively affect our psychological and physical well-being (Martin & Ford, 2018), so get out there and watch some YouTube hilarity (might I suggest the *REACT channel* ... I love their "Try not to laugh" episodes—I fail every time) or check out *Hairy Farmpit Girls* on the social medias for hysterical tales from a goat farm (baby goat pics are a nice bonus).

[8] Sure, you might be thinking that it's weird to name to inanimate objects, and maybe you're thinking that it's also odd to consider writing projects "objects," but hang with me here ...

Lilly and I would respond, "She's great!" On other days, my response would be more like, "Oh, Lillian," while audibly sighing and shaking my fist in the air. Some days, I would talk to her (read: myself), "OK, Lilly, today's the day. Today's the day that you and I work together. Cool? Cool. Glad we're on the same page."[9]

Since beginning this naming practice, I have watched my colleagues and students name their own projects. Observing the ritual of naming a writing project is fascinating. Some go deep and search websites for the history and meaning of names before deciding, while others keep it light and find a *My Little Pony* name for each of their manuscripts. To each their own.

Don't Eat the Whole Pie (Or Even Pretend That Eating the Whole Pie Is Reasonable . . . or Healthy)

Seriously. Most of us wouldn't try to eat the whole pie at once. With 2,368 calories in the average apple pie, consuming the entire thing would be fairly unhealthy. But, a slice? At 296 calories, a slice of pie is a much more reasonable serving. Think of your finished project as the whole pie. And the various steps to the project as the pieces or servings. Write your draft as you might eat a pie. What's manageable? Is your plan too big? Break it down. Too big is overwhelming . . . and unhealthy.

Realistic plans also (er, especially) have realistic timelines. But creating realistic plans with realistic timelines can be difficult. Estimating the needs of a project is difficult without all of the information. For example, in every episode of those home improvement shows where a team of professionals overtake a room in someone's house, the professionals provide the homeowners an estimate of what the improvements would cost, but (spoiler alert!) there's *always* some emergency that also needs repair, costing the poor homeowners an extra *jillion* dollars. Similarly, no matter what I do, it seems like I underestimate the time it will take me to complete a project. EVERYone in my life will attest to this. They all see me try to be on time . . . and then fail because I miscalculated how long the task would take me to finish. However, I usually miscalculated because it took digging into the project for me to see the hidden tasks behind the figurative walls. Fa la la. Adjust. Breathe. Begin again. When deadlines are firm, start by using the *5x Rule*: Take your estimate of how long you think the task will take you and multiply it by 5. This conservative rule helps me to ensure that I am able to break the task down and map out the timeline to (actually) submit on time.

---

[9] "Page"—get it?? Too much? Sorry, never mind.

When I break the plan down, and then continue to adjust my plan, not only are the tasks more realistic, but they also seem like they are much more actionable and achievable. And you might find that you make more progress when you write for 30 minutes each day than when you write for large blocks of time. In a classic study of faculty members with writer's block, Boice (1983) found that academics who wrote three pages per day, five days a week, were more productive than academics who followed their usual writing approach. Similarly, when Boice (1989) observed the writing habits of new tenure-track faculty members, he found that "binge writers" or those who waited for long blocks of time to write wrote less than those who engaged in regular, brief writing sessions.

So, what can you get done in half an hour? I like to keep a list of these actionable items because crossing things off of lists feels amazing.[10] Maybe your list will include outlining or fleshing out components of an outline. Today might be the day that you work on references or perhaps it's the day that you format tables because you just do not have the mental capacity to synthesize the literature. But, one thing is for sure, if you put "finish the literature review today" on your to-do list it's probably not going to get done. Reasonable. Realistic. Make sure you can check off both when you're making your goals (#Flow). Then, when you're done, always make a plan for the specific steps that you will start with next time so that you don't spend (read: waste) time trying to remember where you left off. Every time I walk away from my writing, I note, "START HERE" in the document and follow with my plan of the specific task that needs to be done next.

Making (and Sticking to) a Block Schedule

One of the best ways to ensure that you are able to meet those realistic goals that you set for yourself is to set a block schedule (like high school) and stick to it (ahem, like you did in high school). The trick is to find the best time of the day that works for you. Many writers, including Maya Angelou, Stephen King, Ernest Hemingway, and W. H. Auden,[11] find the first hours of the day the most productive. However, not everyone is a morning lark. Some writers find that their most productive hours are later in the day or perhaps even in the wee hours of the night while many of us are getting our beauty rest.

Of course, having a schedule that aligns to our preferences and circadian rhythms is a luxury not afforded to everyone. Teaching and taking

---

[10] Shout-out to all my fellow list makers out there—anybody else include things like brushing your teeth on your daily to-do list on those days when you're not sure how accomplished you're going to feel?

[11] Interesting Tidbit: Auden had a daily writing routine that ended with a cocktail hour that began at 6:30 p.m. sharp.

classes, going to meetings, or working on other jobs to pay the bills often dictates the available times we have to write. You might find that charting out your responsibilities and to-do list at the beginning of each week helps to identify available chunks of time where you can slot in your writing time (remember that small chunks of time are perfect!). Some find it satisfying to chart their week using an old-school paper calendar, while others set up the chunks of time as events within their electronic calendars.

Now that you have your calendar set up, how do you go about holding your feet to the fire and *actually* sticking with the schedule you created? First, it's important to hold your writing time sacred. Consider it a meeting with yourself (and the project that you just named—maybe even put the project's name on your calendar). When other meetings, people, or events come knocking on your door asking for your time during the time that you set aside for your writing, you will need to have a plan for how you will respond. Notice that I started that last sentence with "when" and not "if." Other meetings, people, and events *will* bid for your time. Your response? "Sorry, I have a meeting at that time." No matter how phony that response seems, it is 100% true. You do have a meeting—the most important kind and with the most important person: you.

Growing Habit Seedlings

Now that you have your sweet block schedule drafted and you're ready to defend it like a feral cat, it's time to examine your writing habit. Let's pretend that your writing habit is a precious little plant seedling that you're trying to grow. When it comes to actual plants, I've learned that I have to buy the brand "Plants of Steel."[12] Clear advertising suggests that Plants of Steel are the easiest to grow/hardest to kill. Indeed, these have been the *only* the plants that don't get murdered in my house. The easiest habits to grow (and keep alive) are those related to easy behaviors and those that occur in stable environments (Fiorella, 2020). When I think of easy behaviors occurring in stable environments, things like driving to work or eating ice cream in bed come to mind. Most unfortunately, writing is not an easy behavior, and our writing/working environments are not always as stable as we'd like. Nonetheless, there is potential to grow our habit seedlings with goals (see earlier strategy section), rewards (see next strategy section), and repetition (Lally & Gardner, 2013; Wood & Neal, 2007; Wood & Rünger, 2016). Here we're going to focus our

---

[12] That's a real brand, y'all.

attention on repetition and consistency and how they can help us create a more sustainable writing practice.

Think: rituals. Rituals can help to make aspects of our environment more stable by providing consistent cues that can trigger our behavior. What's my weirdo writing ritual? Well, I wake up—often like a *white walker* where my eyes spring open in some super creepy way (that's not totally creepy because I'm actually just waking up in the morning). Anyway, after that, I pour a cup of coffee, go to my office, fix the lights exactly so, turn on the computer, turn on the oil diffuser,[13] turn on the space heater under my desk,[14] reread my notes from the last writing session, take two minutes to make any changes to my plan, and get to work. This process helps me fall into flow the fastest. I used to look at my email first thing, but that often got me sucked into the black hole of death—I mean, replies. Instead, I have found the earliest hours of the day to be the ones where I'm apt to make the most writing progress so I save my inbox for another part of the day.

What about you? What's your writing ritual? That is, what does "getting ready to write" look like for you? What are some of the things you do right before you start writing? Do you typically write in the same place? Are there things that need to be "in order" before you begin? After answering these questions, consider how you might adjust your writing ritual to make building your writing habit more likely to happen. Make your ritual pleasant, enjoyable, and one that sets your practice up for progress.

Motivation Check

Establishing an effective motivation system can be the fertilizer to help grow those writing habit seedlings discussed in the last section. The complexity of your personal motivation system is up to you. However, research suggests links between social support and productivity and well-being (Park et al., 2004). For example, one study of management PhD students found faculty support to be the most important factor related to student research productivity (Kim & Karau, 2009). In addition to finding supportive mentors, you might find it helpful to find an *accountabilibuddy* (accountability + buddy), or another person with whom you share your writing goals and progress. Your accountabilibuddy does not need to be in your same field or even in the same place in their program or career—just someone who also wants help staying on track with their writing goals. To

---

[13] *Chill Pill* by Essential Oils is one of my faves.

[14] I tend to need the space heater even in the summer because I have the blood circulation of a corpse.

get started, consider setting a monthly/weekly goal, such as a daily/weekly word/time minimum (e.g., 400 words/day or 1 hour/day). Then, considering your goal, commit to the actions you will take to reach it. How will you make the goal happen? What might get in the way? How might your accountabilibuddy help? Finally, set a regular check-in time and how you'll communicate (e.g., text, email). For more on accountability groups and finding others to support you as you write, see Chapter 8 [Finding Social Support for Writing].

Your motivation system might also include either rewards, punishments, or both. What makes you want to work? When do you work your hardest? What are you working for? Who are you working for? Some find it rewarding to work toward their favorite snack, a chat with a friend, or a stroll through the park or woods. Others celebrate the end of a writing block with a dance mini-session to one of their favorite songs.[15]

Perhaps you find avoiding punishment more motivating. My friend and I recently experimented with this. We each made a challenging, yet realistic, writing goal for the month. Then we bet each other a meaningful amount of money that we would meet our goal. Failure to meet our goal would result in sending the money to a particular politician that we simply could not imagine having our donation (shudder). For the life of me, I cannot remember a deadline being more "motivating," but I likely will not attempt this experiment again, as the combination of a deadline and the visceral reaction I had toward the thought of sending my hard-earned cash money to the politician I despised worsened my anxious feelings. Fellow writers who struggle with writing anxiety should use the punishment-as-a-motivation strategy cautiously.

Like most things, a balanced reward–punishment approach might work best. I have found group writing challenges to be excellent motivators (see the Resources section of this chapter for one of my faves). This strategy is successful for me (and many of other writers) because of the combination of achievable goals, accountabilibuddies, a supportive group, and the promise of a modest reward or not-terribly-painful punishment for meeting or not meeting my goal, respectively. No matter what you choose to motivate your regular writing practice, it's the continued *practice*—the building of a writing habit—that matters most.

---

[15] One of my colleagues suggested the song, "I Will Survive" by Gloria Gaynor at a recent dance mini-session celebration with my virtual writing group. As I busted my moves and listened to the lyrics, I realized just how much of the song could be about my writing project! "Go on now, go, walk out the door . . . "

How Reading, Listening, and Speaking Can Help With Writing

When you're caught in the spin cycle struggling with your draft, try switching up your approach to start moving past your stuck point. Maybe read your draft. Or listen to it with software or an app that reads your documents aloud. There are different apps available that will do this. I use the Voice Dream app on my iOS device, but note that it is not perfect. In fact, it's a bit like listening to a monotone British robot (yawn), but it gets the job done. When I'm stuck in my writing, or trying to maximize my time on my commute to work, I often listen to what I've written in my draft. I find that listening distances me a bit from the draft and can give me a different perspective. While listening, I think about the pieces that seem to be missing or are not yet fitting well. Then I use the dictation and notes features on my phone to record notes that I then email to myself. The best part? Working on my writing in a meaningful way without lifting a pen or starting my computer (I should mention that I totally, and without an ounce of guilt, count this as writing). You might find that using this strategy in a relaxing, but not distracting, location brings the added benefit of peaceful productivity.

I also use dictation software when staring at a blank page or the blinking cursor makes me anxious. Think of this strategy as a brain dump of sorts. We think a lot faster than we type, and sometimes we just need to talk out our ideas. Again, you can use the dictation and notes features on your mobile device to get your ideas on the "page" (that's actually how I'm writing this very section, honestly). Then go back and revise.[16] Reading, listening, and speaking can be useful strategies to try when you are feeling overwhelmed with your writing or you don't know where to start.

A Date With Your Journal

When you find yourself avoiding the work of writing, consider working on your feelings related to the project instead. Journal about how things are going, how you're feeling, what's going well, not so well, or maybe about the objects you would like to throw at your writing. Figure 3.1 shows a passage cut from my own writing journal while I was writing this book. A quick glance at this journal entry shows that I was not necessarily in the best headspace to be productive. Nonetheless,

---

[16] I must mumble because Siri sometimes butchers the words that I so eloquently told her. ("No, Siri, I said, "self-efficacy" not "South Africa." *Sigh*)

Figure 3.1   Passage From My Writing Journal

Ugh.

Today is a struggle. What is standing in the way? What are the major questions that I have? What would the author of this [expletive] book tell me to do? Take my notes from last night's meeting and the hard copy notes I have and put them in place within document. Make your [expletive] plan. Dear mind-[expletive], I see you. I see you and I won't let you win. #AllTheFeelings

---

writing deadlines often do not wait until we are perfectly ready to begin, and journaling can illuminate potential patterns in your thinking about writing.

Don't know what to write? You can always write the same sentence over and over, like, say, "Ideas are going to come to me . . . Ideas are going to come to me," until the ideas *actually* come to you. Sometimes, it's just difficult to get started, and journal writing can provide the behavioral change that can lead to stronger motivation. And, while many types of expressive writing can lead to improved well-being, focusing your expressive writing on finding the positive aspects of negative situations can be especially beneficial (Pennebaker & Chung, 2011).

Vivid Alternative Endings

Engaging in the recall of specific details of events can have positive and significant effects on memory, imagination, problem solving, and psychological well-being (Jing et al., 2016; Madore et al., 2014). In one recent study, Jing et al., (2017) found that vividly thinking about positive alternative outcomes to anticipated negative events helped participants alter the perceptions of those events to be more positive. We can modify the procedures used in the Jing et al., (2017) study to positively alter our sour thoughts about writing. Use the steps below to be both the experimenter *and* the participant in this activity.

1. To begin, write down 1–6 negative future writing scenarios. What is it that could go wrong with your writing projects? These

scenarios should be as specific and concrete as possible. Give each event a title.

2. Using as much detail as possible to describe your thoughts and feelings, imagine experiencing the negative events for 2 minutes each. Each event should last several hours and take place in a specific location.

3. Consider the plausibility of each event you imagined. On a scale of 1 (low) to 9 (high), how likely is this event to occur? Next, rate the valence for each event. On a scale of 1 (extremely bad) to 9 (extremely good), how might this event affect your life?

4. Set a timer and look out your busiest window for one minute. When the minute is up, close your eyes and get a picture in your head about what you saw and heard. Using as much vivid detail as possible, describe the surroundings (What was present in the environment? What did the environment look like?), people (What did they look like? What were they wearing?), and actions (What were the people doing? What happened first, next, last?). Try to be as specific and detailed as you can.

5. Now go back to the negative future writing scenario(s) you generated in Steps 1–2. For each event, take 5 minutes to write out as many positive alternative scenarios as possible. Consider modifying the outcome of the original event (e.g., doing well instead of doing poorly), altering how you feel about the event by emotionally reinterpreting the outcome (e.g., although you didn't do as well as you hoped, it could have been worse), altering how you feel about the consequences (e.g., the writing project is not the most important one of your career), or changing how you interacted with others in the original event (e.g., you learn disappointing news via email rather than in person). For each alternate scenario, keep the core elements of each event constant (e.g., if the event is about a specific writing project, refrain from thinking about other projects), and remember that each alternative scenario should be more positive than the original event.

6. In this step, you're going to repeat Step 3. First, re-rate the plausibility of the original negative future writing scenario(s) you imagined. On a scale of 1 (low) to 9 (high), how likely is this event to occur? Then re-rate the valence for each event. On a scale of 1

(extremely bad) to 9 (extremely good), how might this event affect your life?

7. Finally, consider the plausibility of each alternate event you imagined in Step 5. On a scale of 1 (low) to 9 (high), how likely is this alternative event to occur? Next, rate the valence for each alternative event. On a scale of 1 (extremely bad) to 9 (extremely good), how might this event affect your life?

Now that you've finished the experiment, what do you notice? How do you feel about the original negative writing scenario(s)? Feeling more optimistic?

NEXT STEPS

- ☐ Take note of when you're catastrophizing about your writing. When you find yourself in the funk, take a step back and make a conscious decision to stop feeding into negative self-talk.

- ☐ Practice positive self-talk to have kinder conversations within your own head.

- ☐ Consider naming your project to give your writing (and your relationship with writing) the attention it deserves.

- ☐ Make a reasonable and realistic plan with a reasonable and realistic timeline for your writing. Then revise as necessary.

- ☐ Save time, energy, and frustration! At the end of each writing session, make a plan for the next time you sit down to write.

- ☐ Find a time to write at least once a day (even for 15 minutes!) for five days a week to build your writing habit. Then block out that time on your calendar and keep it sacred.

- ☐ Create a productive writing ritual to help reduce the friction between you and the writing habit and practice you're trying to build.

- ☐ Enlist a friend or colleague to help you stay motivated and hold you accountable for the goals you set for yourself.

- ☐ Consider listening to your draft using software that reads your document aloud. Or use dictation software to "write" your ideas down (#EditLater).

- ☐ Try journaling about your writing feelings. Do you recognize any patterns in your thinking?

- ☐ Close your eyes and use as much detail as possible to vividly imagine an optimistic alternative ending to adjust your negative thoughts about writing.

EXTRA RESOURCES

Make Your Emotional Health Your Priority

If you are having a hard time or need someone to talk to, there are people who care about you and can help. Sites like Psychology Today (https://www.psychologytoday.com/us/therapists) and GoodTherapy (https://www.goodtherapy.org) allow you to find therapists in your area and sort by gender, specialty (e.g., anxiety), accepted insurance, and so on. If making a call or appointment with a professional seems overwhelming, then consider reaching out to a friend or family member. Because academia can sometimes feel like a weird world that only other academics understand, you might find that a classmate/colleague in a similar place as you can especially relate to your feelings.

Barrett-Fox, R. (n.d.). *Any good thing monthly writing challenge.* https://anygoodthing.com/agt-monthly-writing-challenge/

Bolker, J. (1998). *Writing your dissertation in fifteen minutes a day: A guide to starting, revising, and finishing your doctoral thesis.* Holt Paperbacks.

Harris, R. (2008). *The happiness trap: How to stop struggling and start living: A guide to ACT.* KwaZulu-Trumpeter Publishers.

Sweeny, M. (2018). *Zen as f*ck: A journal for practicing the mindful art of not giving a sh*t.* Castle Point Books.

Wilson, S. (2017). *First we make the beast beautiful: A new story about anxiety.* Pan Macmillan.

Quiz: What Does Your Sleeping Position Say About Your Level of Writing Stress?[17]

Choose your go-to sleeping position from the options below. Then read the descriptions to learn insight into the relationship between your snooze style and your writing.

| Fetal | Soldier | Starfish |
| Position | Position | Position |

Fetal Position: Your friends and colleagues may not know it, but your writing goals and to-do lists make your heart race. However, pretending to be back in your mother's womb seems to quell the panic.

Soldier Position: Writing sometimes makes you anxious, but you find that pinning your arms to your sides brings a comforting level of security.

Starfish Position: You are rarely overwhelmed by writing's shenanigans. You fiercely look it in its beady, little writing eyes and say in a voice that rivals only the mother of dragons, "Bring it."

---

[17] Disclaimer: This quiz is ridiculous and in no way scientifically accurate.

Activity: Dress Your Writing Monster

Skip to the perforated pages at the end of the book to cut out the pictures and transform your personal Writing Monster (add color for extra effect). Turns out that a Hawaiian shirt, cargo shorts, and a pair of shades can turn even the most menacing of beasts into a charming beach creature (who knew?!).

References

American Psychological Association [n.d.]. https://www.apa.org/topics/anxiety/

Barreira, P., Basilico, M., & Bolotnyy, V. (2018). *Graduate student mental health: Lessons from American economics departments* [Working Paper].

Boice, B. (1997). Which is more productive, writing in binge patterns of creative illness or in moderation? *Written Communication, 14*(4), 435–459. doi:10.1177/0741088397014004001

Boice, R. (1983). Experimental and clinical treatments of writing blocks. *Journal of Consulting and Clinical Psychology, 51*(2), 183–191. doi:10.1037/0022-006X.51.2.183

Boice, R. (1989). Procrastination, busyness and bingeing. *Behaviour Research and Therapy, 27*(6), 605–611. doi:10.1016/0005-7967(89)90144-7

Boice, R., & Johnson, K. (1984). Perception and practice of writing for publication by faculty at a doctoral-granting university. *Research in Higher Education, 21*(1), 33–43. doi:10.1007/BF00975034

Chemi, T. (2016). *The experience of flow in artistic creation.* In L. Harmat, F. Ørsted Andersen, F. Ullén, J. Wright, & G. Sadlo (Eds.), *Flow experience* (pp. 37–50). Springer.

Csikszentmihalyi, M. (1975). *Beyond boredom and anxiety.* Jossey-Bass.

Csikszentmihalyi, M. (1997). *Finding flow: The psychology of engagement with everyday life.* Basic Books.

Eagleson, C., Hayes, S., Mathews, A., Perman, G., & Hirsch, C. R. (2016). The power of positive thinking: Pathological worry is reduced by thought replacement in generalized anxiety disorder. *Behaviour Research and Therapy, 78*, 13–18. doi:10.1016/j.brat.2015.12.017

Ellis, A. (1962). *Reason and emotion in psychotherapy.* Citadel.

Fiorella, L. (2020). The science of habit and its implications for student learning and well-being. *Educational Psychology Review*, 1–23.

Guthrie, S., Lichten, C. A., Van Belle, J., Ball, S., Knack, A., & Hofman, J. (2018). Understanding mental health in the research environment: A rapid evidence assessment. *Rand Health Quarterly, 7*(3), 2.

Hoehn-Saric, R., & McLeod, D. R. (1988). The peripheral sympathetic nervous system: Its role in normal and pathologic anxiety. *Psychiatric Clinics of North America, 11*(2), 375–386.

Huerta, M., Goodson, P., Beigi, M., & Chlup, D. (2017). Graduate students as academic writers: Writing anxiety, self-efficacy and emotional intelligence. *Higher Education Research & Development, 36*(4), 716–729. doi:10.1080/07294360.2016.1238881

Jing, H. G., Madore, K. P., & Schacter, D. L. (2016). Worrying about the future: An episodic specificity induction impacts problem solving, reappraisal, and well-being. *Journal of Experimental Psychology: General, 145*(4), 402–418. doi:10.1037/xge0000142

Jing, H. G., Madore, K. P., & Schacter, D. L. (2017). Preparing for what might happen: An episodic specificity induction impacts the generation of alternative future events. *Cognition, 169*, 118–128. doi:10.1016/j.cognition.2017.08.010

Kim, K., & Karau, S. J. (2009). Working environment and the research productivity of doctoral students in management. *Journal of Education for Business, 85*(2), 101–106. doi:10.1080/08832320903258535

Lally, P., & Gardner, B. (2013). Promoting habit formation. *Health Psychology Review, 7*(sup 1), S137–S158.

Madore, K. P., Gaesser, B., & Schacter, D. L. (2014). Constructive episodic simulation: Dissociable effects of a specificity induction on remembering, imagining, and describing in young and older adults. *Journal of Experimental Psychology: Learning, Memory, and Cognition, 40*(3), 609–622.

Martin, R. A., & Ford, T. (2018). *The psychology of humor: An integrative approach* (2nd ed.). Academic Press.

Martinez, C. T., Kock, N., & Cass, J. (2011). Pain and pleasure in short essay writing: Factors predicting university students' writing anxiety and writing self-efficacy. *Journal of Adolescent & Adult Literacy, 54*(5), 351–360. doi:10.1598/JAAL.54.5.5

Nakamura, J., & Csikszentmihalyi, M. (2014). *The concept of flow.* In *Flow and the foundations of positive psychology* (pp. 239–263). Springer.

Nolen-Hoeksema, S., Wisco, B. E., & Lyubomirsky, S. (2008). Rethinking rumination. *Perspectives on Psychological Science, 3*(5), 400–424. doi:10.1111/j.1745-6924.2008.00088.x

Onwuegbuzie, A. J. (1999). Writing apprehension among graduate students: Its relationship to self-perceptions. *Psychological Reports, 84*(3), 1034–1039. doi:10.2466/pr0.1999.84.3.1034

Park, K.-O., Wilson, M. G., & Lee, M. S. (2004). Effects of social support at work on depression and organizational productivity. *American Journal of Health Behavior, 28*(5), 444–455. doi:10.5993/AJHB.28.5.7

Pekrun, R. (2006). The control-value theory of achievement emotions: Assumptions, corollaries, and implications for educational research and practice. *Educational Psychology Review, 18*(4), 315–341. doi:10.1007/s10648-006-9029-9

Pennebaker, J. W., & Chung, C. K. (2011). *Expressive writing and its links to mental and physical health.* In H. S. Friedman (Ed.), *Oxford handbook of health psychology* (pp. 417–437). Oxford University Press.

Perry, S. K. (1999). *Writing in flow: Keys to enhanced creativity.* Writer's Digest Books.

Salzberg, S. (2019, February 7).https://www.sharonsalzberg.com

Skodzik, T., Leopold, A., & Ehring, T. (2017). Effects of a training in mental imagery on worry: A proof-of-principle study. *Journal of Anxiety Disorders, 45,* 24–33. doi:10.1016/j.janxdis.2016.11.009

Wachholz, P., & Etheridge, C. (1996). Writing self-efficacy beliefs of high- and low-apprehensive writers. *Journal of Developmental Education, 19*(3), 16–24.

Wellington, J. (2010). More than a matter of cognition: An exploration of affective writing problems of post-graduate students and their possible solutions. *Teaching in Higher Education, 15*(2), 135–150. doi:10.1080/13562511003619961

Willingham, D. T., Hughes, E. M., & Dobolyi, D. G. (2015). The scientific status of learning styles theories. *Teaching of Psychology, 42*(3), 266–271. doi:10.1177/0098628315589505

Wood, W., & Neal, D. T. (2007). A new look at habits and the habit-goal interface. *Psychological Review, 114*(4), 843–863.

Wood, W., & Rünger, D. (2016). Psychology of habit. *Annual Review of Psychology, 67,* 289–314.

Writing Self-Efficacy

"The moment you doubt whether you can fly, you cease for ever to be able to do it."

—J. M. Barrie, *Peter Pan in Kensington Gardens*

Understanding the Psychology

Sure, Peter Pan was a creepy little kidnapper who used his flying skills to hustle into nurseries at night, but you have to admit—Pan's unrelenting belief in his own cleverness was rather impressive. Wouldn't it be lovely if we could face our writing with the fearlessness that Peter faced angry pirates or hungry crocodiles? Such fearlessness aligns with the psychological concept of *self-efficacy*, or the belief that one can be successful at a specific task (Bandura, 1997). Decades of research highlight the influential role self-efficacy beliefs can play on our writing success. Those with higher writing efficacy often enjoy writing more (Collie et al., 2016), experience less anxiety while writing (Huerta et al., 2017), and are more strategic and successful than those with lower writing efficacy beliefs (Ekholm et al., 2015; Shell et al., 1989; Zumbrunn et al., 2019). In fact, self-efficacy is often a much more potent predictor of success than one's actual ability (Bandura & Estes, 1977; Bandura, 1997; Zimmerman, 2000). I'm going to say that again because it's one of the most important things that you'll read in this book: Self-efficacy is often a much more potent predictor of success than one's actual ability. That might sound absurd, but if you think about it, it makes sense. If we do not believe that we will be successful at a specific task, then we are less likely to approach that task, won't try as hard during the task, will be less persistent when the going gets tough, and for these reasons, will likely be less productive and ultimately less successful—*even when we have the ability to be successful.* That is powerful.

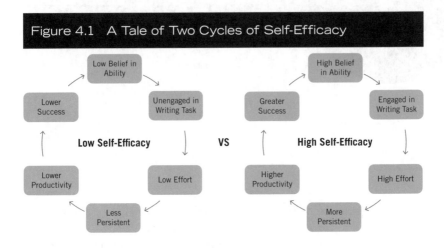

Figure 4.1 A Tale of Two Cycles of Self-Efficacy

As an example, let's look at Figure 4.1, which shows two versions of the cycle of self-efficacy. On the left is the cycle of low self-efficacy. If I'm a student in PhD-Land and I do not believe I can complete my dissertation, I might avoid writing (and won't experience success that way—in fact, I will experience feelings of failure that will just reinforce my already low-efficacy beliefs). Even if I do take on the necessary writing, I am less likely to put in the level of effort that matches my ability, and I might wander off into the comfortable blue expanse of the Twitterverse when I reach a hurdle. Altogether, I will then be less productive and won't experience the success necessary for boosting my self-efficacy. And the tragic cycle begins again, ad infinitum.

Fortunately, the cycle of self-efficacy can also be positive and empowering where feelings of efficacy lead to accomplishment. This cycle is illustrated on the right side of Figure 4.1. When we feel on top of our writing game, we are much more likely to jump into what needs to be done in the draft, put in the required time and effort, adaptively manage the stumbling blocks along the way, and end up with a done draft, a self–high–five, and the belief that we can similarly crush the next writing goal on our list. Raise your hand if that makes you swoon just a little.

What causes us to get caught in a cycle of *can't and won't* rather than *can and will*? For starters, the final hurdle of the dissertation is unquestionably difficult for students. It requires a level of independence for which many feel unprepared (Lovitts, 2008; Varney, 2010). Similarly, new faculty or faculty new to a research topic, genre, or methodology might not feel prepared for steep incline of the learning curve. If we understand the factors that contribute to self-efficacy, we are much more prepared to be confident badasses ready to take on our writing, no matter the slope of the learning curve. There are four primary sources that predict how efficacious we feel toward writing tasks: mastery experiences, vicarious experiences, feedback or social persuasion, and physiological responses (Bandura, 1997; Pajares et al., 2007). The following sections provide the skinny on each of these sources.

Mastery Experiences: Failing Up

Out of all the factors that contribute to our efficacy beliefs, mastery experience is perhaps the most influential (Usher & Pajares, 2008). In a nutshell, mastery experiences are the interpreted results of our prior experiences engaging in a task. Success and failure are inherent components of mastery experiences and so are the judgments we make about those results. For example, Kala crushed framing out the methods section of her thesis, this construed success making her feel a higher sense of self-efficacy for writing. On the other hand, Elijah struggled every time he started to write the introduction of his manuscript, this interpreted failure leading to lower writing efficacy beliefs.

Of course, we'd all rather have successful mastery experiences than failure mastery experiences. However, at least some failure is inevitable in the game of learning. Students and faculty alike often realize all too quickly that rejection and botched plans are rampant in academia.[1] The trick is in how we deal with failure. I'm not saying that you should pretend that it doesn't sting. Failing usually isn't super fun. However, recognizing what you learned from each task that didn't go exactly the way you had planned can help with keeping perspective. Maybe you learned that your writing goal wasn't as reasonable or realistic as you intended. Or, perhaps you weren't as productive as you thought you'd be writing in your cozy bed.[2] Reframing your missteps from the perspective of learning and growth can give you clues as to what you might try differently the next time you pick up your pen.

In addition to managing failure in more productive ways, you can also set yourself up to endure fewer failures by giving yourself plenty of practice within a supportive environment. There are two key words in that last phrase—*practice* and *supportive*. Let's dig into both.

---

[1] Oh, hey, Reviewer 2. And, what's up, null findings! How've you been?! *Nods curtly to grant rejection in the corner of the room*

[2] If you're writing or studying in bed, you seriously need to clean up your sleep hygiene. For more on understanding the links between healthy sleep, well-being, and productivity, check out the book, *The Promise of Sleep* (Dement & Vaughan, 1999).

First, as discussed in Chapter 2 [Imposter Syndrome and Writer Identity], it takes heaps of practice to develop writing skills. Like a lot. We're not talking about casual and occasional practice here. No, we're talking about planned and thoughtful regular practice that is appropriately matched with our ability. Remember Elijah, who struggled to write a compelling introduction? Elijah might need to snuggle up with his draft every day (even if only for a small amount of time) and write—and rewrite, and potentially rewrite—several introductory paragraphs, thinking carefully along the way about what's working and what isn't.

Such practice is not easy to establish alone. You guessed it—this is where the supportive environment comes in. Guided mastery can provide the means necessary for increasing resiliency and self-efficacy (Bandura, 1997). In other words, when writers are aligned with supportive others who provide a sense of community, help them determine appropriate goals, and coach them on the use of effective strategies to meet their goals, they are more apt to cope with disappointment in their writing and build healthier writing efficacy beliefs. Visit Chapter 8 [Finding Social Support for Writing] for a detailed discussion on building a supportive village for you and your writing.

Vicarious Experiences: The Comparison Trap

Learning from observations of others, or vicarious experiences, can also inform our self-efficacy beliefs. In our studies and in our careers, we're desperate to do the right thing. To ensure that we are, in fact, getting it right, we often compare who we are, what we're thinking, what we're writing, and what we're doing[3] to the thoughts and behaviors of others. We compare to see if our results are in the ballpark of where we believe we're supposed to be. These comparisons can lead us to lots of the feels—from satisfaction, pride, and happiness when we feel like we measure up, to doubts, disappointment, envy, and despair when we believe we've missed the mark.

When it comes to writing, there is no shortage of people or material against which we can judge ourselves. Students in graduate school compare their writing to that of their peers and faculty mentors in their program as well as the legion of papers and books they read as part of their studies. And, it isn't all that different for those who cross the bridge to Faculty Land. Career academics often need not look further than their bookshelves or across the hall for evidence of writing success. Regularly,

---

[3] And what we look like, but we'll save that topic for a different book.

these comparison models showcase expertise or shiny, polished bushels of writing, but observing others who struggle through writing tasks until they are successful can lead to healthier writing beliefs. In one study, participants who watched a writer struggle but ultimately improve her writing technique outperformed their peers who watched a writer whose performance was flawless (Zimmerman & Kitsantas, 2002). Regrettably, opportunities to witness others wrestle with their writing are rare in academia, as there are several who think that the first rule of academic fight club is to keep your struggles to yourself. Struggling in private serves pretty much no one. Being mindful of the hard work, gazillion drafts, and rounds of rejection[4] that likely went into the finished product that you're judging your writing against is one way to help you keep perspective. And do me a favor and be the brave one to share your writing struggles with others—your colleagues, the homies who look up to you, and your own psyche will thank you for it.[5]

Social Persuasion: Flattery and Scars

The feedback we get on our writing can either boost or squash our spirits and our self-efficacy. Whereas specific, encouraging feedback on our progress can sound like someone is playing our fight song, discouraging feedback can resonate like the sad love song that we use to cry ourselves to sleep. Everyone has gotten feedback they remember. Perhaps your mentor complimented the excellent structure and flow of your last draft. Or maybe a reviewer wrote that the ideas in your manuscript were both uninteresting and unsupported . . . womp.

When it comes to feedback, the importance of the writing project or the relationship you have with the person providing the feedback matters. For example, you might value feedback on the 758th class paper you wrote less than you would the feedback you receive on your doctoral thesis, which feels a lot like your unborn child. Similarly, critical feedback from Joe, your annoying peer who has an ill-informed opinion about everything,[6] likely stings a lot less than receiving the same critical feedback from someone you admire (e.g., your academic crush in the field) or someone with power (e.g., your academic adviser or mentor). No doubt, these significant memories can make a lasting

---

[4] Famous Failings: Twelve publishers rejected J. K. Rowling's first *Harry Potter* manuscript, 27 publishing houses rejected John Grisham's first book, and 30 publishers snubbed *Carrie* by Stephen King.

[5] Check out anything from one of my sheroes, Brené Brown, to learn more about the power of bravery and vulnerability.

[6] Uh, thanks, Joe. Next. *Swipes left*

impression on our self-efficacy, but it's the feedback we receive over and over again that can shape our efficacy beliefs even more.

It's hard for anyone to hear that they didn't do something exactly right, but it's important to not get caught in the comments section of your draft. Remember that no matter who the feedback is from, it doesn't define you, your writing, or your future. To help keep perspective, you might begin by highlighting every piece of positive feedback.[7] End there, too—rereading those positive comments can keep your focus on the encouragement you receive. Then, consider focusing on the specific suggestions that can help you improve. It's important to look for consistency across messages. For example, if several readers tell you to simplify your language to improve the clarity of your writing,[8] then maybe that's something for you to think about. For a detailed discussion on how feedback = ♥, see Chapter 7 [Embracing the Feedback Process].

Physiological Responses: Intense Feedback From Your Bod

From fatigue and mood to stress and anxiety, sometimes it's our bodies that send us messages about whether or not we should feel efficacious about our ideas or writing. Similar to our salient experiences with receiving feedback from others, these messages can pack a powerful punch. For instance, I can remember the very first time I presented my ideas and writing at a national academic conference. I had never been to a conference before, let alone presented at one, and I had exactly zero ideas about what to expect. A few colleagues of mine told me not to worry about it—that there would only be about 20 people and all I had to do was talk to them about my research. No big deal. I showed up and there was standing room only— about 50 to 100 people! To top it off, I had to follow a ridiculously eloquent researcher from a mega prestigious university. When it was my turn, I was so anxious that my knees were literally knocking. And when I looked out into the crowd, all I saw were looks of deep sympathy. *Oh, God.* I knew I was bombing it and my heart was racing. My body was sending my brain the signal to run. *Get out of here, lady, you are seriously out of your league!*

---

[7] Unfortunately, not all drafts will come back to you with encouraging nuggets of praise—they should, but it sometimes doesn't happen. Why? Well, some reviewers are jerks. Other reviewers aren't jerks, but they were in too big a rush to reread their feedback and didn't realize the harshness of their language. Others still aren't necessarily jerks, but they weren't trained on how to give feedback. See Chapter 7 [Embracing the Feedback Process] for some tips to give them on the sly or not so sly.

[8] Including words like *utilize*, *promulgate*, and *erroneous* might get the side-eye from a reader. For help using plain English, see Strunk and White's (1972) timeless classic *The Elements of Style* or the helpful site http://www.plainenglish.co.uk/the-a-z-of-alternative-words.html#P.

Physiologically, bodies can send us messages for our minds to interpret and these include the pace of our heart rate and breath, the sweat on our palms or in our pits, the speed at which our knees knock, or the shade of rosy on our cheeks (Jacobs, 2001). These, my friends, are clear messages. Messages that scream, *Stop what you are doing. Something is terribly wrong.* But, recall from the last chapter [Writing Stress and Anxiety] that there is the possibility of another part of the body at play here—the imagination. Indeed, it was after the presentation—and after a long, healthy cry in a restroom stall—when I first learned of catastrophizing, aka, your overactive, Negative Nelly imagination at work (see Chapter 3 [Writing Stress and Anxiety] for more on catastrophizing).[9]

If, while thinking about your academic ideas or writing, every sign in your body is screaming, *RUN!*—then maybe you need to run. But, this might instead be the moment you need to pause and stay. Stay and consider why your body wants you to run. What are you afraid of? What's the worst that can happen? Like, the actual worst that could happen? This is an opportunity for growth. If you can stay, it's a chance for you to lean in and potentially stretch your self-efficacy.

Our moods also can play a role in how efficacious we feel about our writing. The days I jump out of bed ready to rock my writing have a tendency to put me in a super awesome mood and I coincidentally find that I have a fairly healthy sense of self-efficacy for the writing goals that I'm tackling that day. On the other hand, my writing self-efficacy often takes a hit on the days that I find myself dreading writing. Albert Bandura, perhaps most famous for his Bobo doll experiments observing the effects of exposure to violence on children's throwdown behavior (1961), is also the king of self-efficacy.[10] Bandura (1997) suggests that we tend to function the best when our physiological arousal is neither too high nor too low. So, too, does my homie, Mihaly Csikszentmihalyi (1997)[11], the godfather of creativity, happiness, and flow (see Chapter 3 [Writing Stress and Anxiety] for more on flow).

---

[9] This was also the time when a "friend" told me that next time I should *imagine the audience naked.* Um, that was some of the weirdest advice I ever received, so I won't give you the same nonsense. I mean, consider how horribly wrong such an exercise could go. *Yikes.*

[10] Note: I'm very biased. My dog's middle name is Bandura. Literally.

[11] Pronounced "*Me-high Cheek-sent-me-high*"

TL;DR Summary

- Writing self-efficacy, or the belief that we can be successful at writing tasks, is a powerful force in whether or not we are actually successful in our writing.

- The cycle of self-efficacy can be really incredible or really terrible. When we feel efficacious about our writing, we are more likely to approach our writing tasks in the first place, put in more effort, persist longer, and be more successful in those writing tasks, which then leads to higher efficacy beliefs. On the other hand, low writing self-efficacy can lead us to avoid our writing, put in little effort and persistence, and be less successful, which reinforces our already low efficacy beliefs.

- There are four primary sources that predict our level of writing self-efficacy: mastery experiences, vicarious experiences, social persuasion, and physiological responses.

- Mastery experiences are our interpretations of the results from our experiences engaging in writing tasks (aka, successes and failures) and tend to be the most influential source of self-efficacy. Managing failure in productive ways and giving yourself opportunities for practice in a supportive environment can help you make the most of your mastery experiences.

- Our observations of the successes and failures of others, or vicarious experiences, can also inform our writing efficacy beliefs. It's impossible not to notice how others are doing with their writing, but be careful not to fall into the comparison trap, otherwise known as *the lair of compare and despair.*

- When it comes to writing, the source of social persuasion often comes in the form of feedback, and this feedback can be uplifting, depressing, and anything in-between. Use feedback for what it's worth—and be careful about how much power you give it.

- Our bodies send us messages in the form of physiological responses (e.g., fatigue, mood, heart rate), and our minds can

Continued

interpret these messages as signals of whether or not we should feel efficacious about our writing. As you learned in the last chapter, recognizing these responses is the first step in taking control of their effect on your efficacy—and your writing.

Essential Strategies for Productive (and Sane) Writing

It's ratty to feel like we can't write. Fortunately, research shows that we can boost our sense of efficacy by focusing on the four sources that contribute to these beliefs. Get to work by choosing one to two strategies from the following sections to start fostering a stronger sense of writing self-efficacy.

Tracking Gratitude and Wins

Writing can be tough and when it's tough, it's easy for our efficacy beliefs to take a nosedive. Worse, these negative beliefs can hijack our productivity and hold our progress hostage. However, the opposite—gratitude—can have a much more positive effect on our well-being and productivity (Wood et al., 2010). In one recent study of UK academics, grateful individuals had higher ratings of subjective well-being, positive affect, and overall mental health than their less grateful peers (Darabi et al., 2017). Using progress charts can also boost writing self-efficacy, productivity, and success (García & de Caso, 2006). At the end of each writing session, take two minutes to name and celebrate your gratitude for your writing or the successes you experienced. Was a reviewer particularly helpful? Were you able to find 15 minutes to write amidst a packed day of classes or meetings? Did you dominate one of your goals? Continue writing even when it felt like it was slowly killing you? Find the perfect reference? The smaller the achievement the better, as it can be validating to see just how many things are going well. This strategy might take some practice, especially if you're having a particularly funky day with your writing. However, you might find that it's the days that we're deep in the funk that we need to celebrate our mini-wins as much as possible.

Some track their progress using a shared spreadsheet and find that doing so helps keep them accountable to their writing goals and development. Keep an eye on how this practice works for you, as it's easy for competition—and all the destructive forces and feels that can accompany competition—to sneak into your process. Privately graphing your success can keep you in your

Figure 4.2 Progress Tracking Board

own lane, comparing your new writing progress to your old self. Figure 4.2 shows a private graph that I keep for myself, which is a board that tracks the progress of each of my writing projects (e.g., journal articles, book chapters, conference presentations, grant proposals). The board is organized into the following sections: in progress, under review, and accepted. I've also used boards that broke down projects into finer-grained categories (e.g., conceptualization, data collection, data analysis, drafting, under review, and accepted). Each writing project is assigned a sticky note and placed on the board in the appropriate section (see Chapter 3 [Writing Stress and Anxiety] for details about how I name my projects). As the project progresses, I move the sticky note across the board. I find it wildly validating to physically move a sticky note from the drafting to under review section or from the under review to accepted section. To track my smaller wins, I list the writing tasks that I plan to tackle for the week and cross them off as I go (see Chapter 3 for more on creating realistic goals).

Keep Your Finger on the Affective Pulse

Awareness and strategic control or the ways in which we approach our writing are important factors of writing success (Zimmerman & Risemberg, 1997). Similar to logging your writing gratitude and progress, tracking your affective responses to writing can also help you keep perspective. One tool designed for use with academic writers of all ages is *RoboCogger* (www.RoboCogger.com), which allows users to set specific goals for their writing projects, graph their feelings about writing, see how their affect changes over time, and keep an electronic journal documenting the reasons underlying their writing affect/mood. Regularly tracking your affective responses to writing can help you recognize patterns in your writing thoughts and behaviors. When those patterns look like a map of Negativeville, such recognition can be a catalyst for change.

Kill Your Darlings

What might happen if you've been working on your writing project for what feels like 87 hours/days/years and it's good—like *real* good. It's beautiful. A work of art, even. You submit it for review. Now, let's imagine that you then receive a misfortune cookie in the form of feedback that you need to cut your most favorite section.[12] This feedback might leave you wondering if your reviewer misread your draft. *Wait. What?! Cut that part?! THAT'S THE BEST PART! Reviewer, how can you be so dense and ruthless!*

Sometimes, when we feel emotionally attached to our words, it's because we don't think we will be able to come up with something better. After all, those two pages of writing might have taken us an eternity to draft so it isn't a stretch to think that the same effort (and maybe pain) will likely go into creating different words should those words get cut. This line of thinking stems from low self-efficacy, or the problem of *can't*. However,

---

[12] The section you almost mailed home to be hung proudly on the fridge.

keep in mind that your brilliant thoughts came to you once. Why wouldn't they come to you again? Why would you think that you would only be able to think of those thoughts that one special time?

Many well-known writers refer to the words, phrases, sentences, or sections that they are most proud of as *darlings*. And, similar to other beloved things in our lives, we tend to lose our sense of objectivity when it comes to our darlings.[13] You simply can't bear to let them go, even if it means keeping them makes your writing unclear or unreadable. It's unacceptable to hold on to writing that muddies the message or confuses your reader. This is when you need to *kill your darlings*.[14] Or, I rather prefer the phrase, *maim your darlings*.[15] Maim them by cutting them out of your current draft and pasting those sweet beloveds into a separate document so that they're not gone forever. Who knows, maybe you revisit them and use the gems in another draft. Or maybe they'll quietly drift off to Word Heaven.

Pump Up the Jam

While it may be no substitute for strong efficacy beliefs, research suggests that music can make you feel stronger and ready to take on your writing. In a recent study, researchers found that listening to power-inducing music[16] activated listeners to feel more powerful and in control (Hsu et al., 2015). Findings also showed that music with more bass lead to the greatest effects. So, what tunes might make you feel like you could run a marathon or arm wrestle someone three times your size? Maybe the theme song from *Rocky*? Death metal? Rap classics from the 90's? Whatever it may be, figure it out and put those jams on blast to start your writing session with a personal pep rally.[17] Then, choose the tunes that keep you writing—or even go sans tunes if that makes the words more easily flow.

---

[13] You know, like those raggedy slippers that should have been replaced ages ago, but you just can't.

[14] The phrase, *kill your darlings*, was originally coined by William Faulkner but popularized by Stephen King.

[15] Killing and maiming?! Too violent? Probably, but work with me for a minute . . .

[16] Songs were pretested and rated by how powerful, dominant, and determined they made listeners feel. High-power music pieces used in the study included: *We Will Rock You* (Queen), *Get Ready for This* (2 Unlimited), and *In Da Club* (50 Cent); low-power music pieces included: *Because We Can* (Fatboy Slim), *Who Let the Dogs Out* (Baha Men), and *Big Poppa* (Notorious B.I.G.).

[17] My personal writing pep rallies include the following steps: Sigh. Rap music. Coffee. Stretch. Breathe. Begin.

NEXT STEPS

☐ Use a progress chart to track your writing gratitude and successes to help keep your focus on the positive mastery experiences you have with writing.

☐ Name and celebrate your wins at the end of every writing session.

☐ Track the way writing makes you feel from day to day. What do you notice about the patterns? Make a plan to change if needed.

☐ Be mindful of your attachment to your writing. Low writing self-efficacy can show up in the form of over-attachment to your drafted words and a loss of your sense of objectivity. Don't be afraid to make cuts to your drafts. Try putting cut sections into a separate document to return to later . . . or not.

☐ Have a pep rally to kick your writing session into high gear. Make a playlist of the songs that make you feel like you can float like a butterfly and sting like a bee. Take a deep breath and play those jams on repeat to help you feel like your most powerful writing self.

EXTRA RESOURCES

Huerta, M., Goodson, P., Beigi, M., & Chlup, D. (2017). Graduate students as academic writers: Writing anxiety, self-efficacy and emotional intelligence. *Higher Education Research & Development, 36*(4), 716–729.

Sincero, J. (2013). *You are a badass: How to stop doubting your greatness and start living an awesome life.* Running Press Adult.

Sincero, J. (2016). *You are a badass talking button (mixed media product).* Running Press Adult.[18]

Usher, E. L., & Pajares, F. (2008). Sources of self-efficacy in school: Critical review of the literature and future directions. *Review of Educational Research, 78*(4), 751–796.

---

[18] Y'all, you need this button. I have one on my desk, and whenever I get a whiff of low self-efficacy while I'm talking with a student or colleague, I silently push the button toward them and nod, signaling for them to push it. Pushing the button results in the lovely author Jen Sincero shouting encouraging phrases that fill the hallway around my office. I'm pretty sure hearing the loud, *"You. Are. A. Badass."* provides not only the student or colleague in front of me, but also my office neighbors and passersby, with a bit of an efficacy boost.

HUMOR BREAK

Quiz: This Sorting Quiz Will Tell You Which Harry Potter Character Describes Your Writing Self-Efficacy[19]

Complete the following quiz to determine the strength of your self-efficacy.

1. You've just received feedback from a reviewer so harsh that it felt like a howler. What do you do?

   A. Yikes. Like that friend who's a wee bit extra, I take a break from it. When I come back to it, I figure out what's useful.
   B. I print it out and burn it like the cursed trash it is.
   C. I put it in a box under my bed . . . with my manuscript. I never look at or mention either again.

2. Which of the following most accurately describes your relationship with writing?

   A. I heart writing! Bring on the writing! All the writing!
   B. I tend to have both good and bad days with writing. It depends on the project and my mood. And the weather. And what I had for breakfast. And divination predictions. And . . .
   C. Writing is not-so-secretly trying to kill me. *nervously looks over shoulder*

3. Which of your writing skills are you most proud of?

   A. Oooh, good question . . . hard to choose, hard to choose. Do I have to choose?
   B. I can craft a mean title page. Then there's bibliography formatting—I crush it every time.
   C. Does reading count as writing? My reading skills are kind of magical.

4. What do you need to write?

   A. I can write with anything, anywhere. I once wrote an entire manuscript in the sand of my favorite beach using only a twig of driftwood.
   B. I write my best with pens made of mystical unicorn hair or phoenix feathers.
   C. I need all the magic—dark and otherwise—to write on most days.

---

[19] Disclaimer: This quiz is ridiculous and in no way scientifically accurate.

MOSTLY A's: Hermione Granger: When it comes to writing, you're a no-non-sense boss who knows you can take charge. Your sick organizational skills, love for learning, and fearlessness for asking questions keep your writing game—and your writing self-efficacy—strong. You keep your writing readily in a pocket-sized Moleskin wherever you go. After all, you never know when a social gathering will become tiresome and nothing gives you the jolt that writing does.

MOSTLY B's: Harry Potter: Sure, you live under the stairs at your aunt and uncle's house, but brewing inside you is a special kind of fierceness. For writing, obviously. With the help of your friends and consistent practice, you begin to believe in your writing ability over time. These beliefs help you defeat the Dark Lord, [Title of Your Dissertation/Manuscript/Grant Proposal].

MOSTLY C's: Neville Longbottom: Yes, your shadow makes you jump, but nothing makes you more nervy than writing. Your lower self-efficacy keeps you from quickly becoming the superstar writer that Professor McGonagall knows you can be. However, here and there you show bouts of real confidence, like that time you took your crush, Writing, to the Snow Ball. Or the time you took charge of the Dark Arts writing club when the leaders went on leave. Perhaps your finest moment of self-efficacy was when you destroyed Voldemort's final horcrux, your thesis, which you aptly named, Nagini the snake.

Activity: A Choose-Your-Own Writing Self-Efficacy Adventure
SO YOU WANT TO BE AN ACADEMIC WRITER?

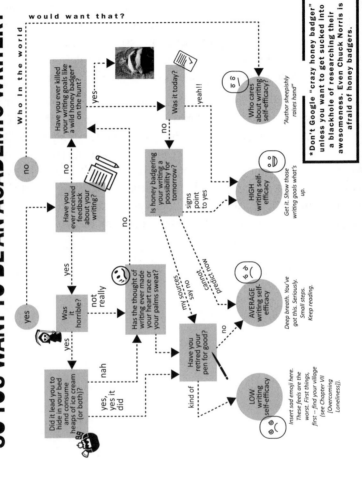

Credit Line: iStock/Sudowoodo, iStock/Amornism, iStock/bsd555, iStock/Penti-Stock, iStock/Freder, iStock/Gunay Abdullayeva

References

Bandura, A. (1997). Self-efficacy: The exercise of control. *W.H. Freeman and Company*.

Bandura, A., & Estes, W. K. (1977). Self-efficacy: Toward a unifying theory of behavioral change. *Psychological Review, 84*(2), 191–215. doi:10.1037/0033-295X.84.2.191

Barrie, J. M. (1906). *Peter Pan in Kensington Gardens*. Hodder & Stoughton.

Collie, R. J., Martin, A. J., & Curwood, J. S. (2016). Multidimensional motivation and engagement for writing: Construct validation with a sample of boys. *Educational Psychology, 36*(4), 771–791. doi:10.1080/01443410.2015.1093607

Csikszentmihalyi, M. (1997). *Finding flow: The psychology of engagement with everyday life*. Basic Books.

Darabi, M., Macaskill, A., & Reidy, L. (2017). Stress among UK academics: Identifying who copes best. *Journal of Further and Higher Education, 41*(3), 393–412. doi:10.1080/0 309877X.2015.1117598

Dement, W. C., & Vaughan, C. (1999). *The promise of sleep: A pioneer in sleep medicine explores the vital connection between health, happiness, and a good night's sleep*. Dell Publishing Co.

Ekholm, E., Zumbrunn, S., & Conklin, S. (2015). The relation of college student self-efficacy toward writing and writing self-regulation aptitude: Writing feedback perceptions as a mediating variable. *Teaching in Higher Education, 20*(2), 197–207. doi:10.1080/13562517.2014.974026

García, J. N., & de Caso, A. M. (2006). Changes in writing self-efficacy and writing products and processes through specific training in the self-efficacy beliefs of students with learning disabilities. *Learning Disabilities: A Contemporary Journal, 4*(2), 1–27.

Hsu, D. Y., Huang, L., Nordgren, L. F., Rucker, D. D., & Galinsky, A. D. (2015). The music of power: Perceptual and behavioral consequences of powerful music. *Social Psychological and Personality Science, 6*(1), 75–83.

Huerta, M., Goodson, P., Beigi, M., & Chlup, D. (2017). Graduate students as academic writers: Writing anxiety, self-efficacy and emotional intelligence. *Higher Education Research & Development, 36*(4), 716–729. doi:10.1080/07294360.2016.1238881

Jacobs, G. D. (2001). The physiology of mind–body interactions: The stress response and the relaxation response. *The Journal of Alternative and Complementary Medicine, 7*(Suppl. 1), 83–92. doi:10.1089/107555301753393841

Lovitts, B. E. (2008). The transition to independent research: Who makes it, who doesn't, and why. *The Journal of Higher Education, 79*(3), 296–325. doi:10.1080/002215 46.2008.11772100

Pajares, F., Johnson, M. J., & Usher, E. L. (2007). Sources of writing self-efficacy beliefs of elementary, middle, and high school students. *Research in the Teaching of English, 42*(1), 104–120.

Shell, D. F., Murphy, C. C., & Bruning, R. H. (1989). Self-efficacy and outcome expectancy mechanisms in reading and writing achievement. *Journal of Educational Psychology, 81*(1), 91–100. doi:10.1037/0022-0663.81.1.91

Strunk, W., & White, E. B. (1972). *The elements of style.* Macmillan.

Usher, E. L., & Pajares, F. (2008). Sources of self-efficacy in school: Critical review of the literature and future directions. *Review of Educational Research, 78*(4), 751–796. doi:10.3102/0034654308321456

Varney, J. J. (2010). The role of dissertation self-efficacy in increasing dissertation completion: Sources, effects and viability of a new self-efficacy construct. *College Student Journal, 44*(4), 932–948.

Wood, A. M., Froh, J. J., & Geraghty, A. W. A. (2010). Gratitude and well-being: A review and theoretical integration. *Clinical Psychology Review, 30*(7), 890–905. doi:10.1016/j.cpr.2010.03.005

Zimmerman, B. J. (2000). Self-efficacy: An essential motive to learn. *Contemporary Educational Psychology, 25*(1), 82–91. doi:10.1006/ceps.1999.1016

Zimmerman, B. J., & Kitsantas, A. (2002). Acquiring writing revision and self-regulatory skill through observation and emulation. *Journal of Educational Psychology, 94*(4), 660–668. doi:10.1037/0022-0663.94.4.660

Zimmerman, B. J., & Risemberg, R. (1997). Becoming a self-regulated writer: A social cognitive perspective. *Contemporary Educational Psychology, 22*(1), 73–101. doi:10.1006/ceps.1997.0919

Zumbrunn, S., Broda, M., Varier, D., & Conklin, S. (2019). Examining the multidimensional role of self-efficacy for writing on student writing self-regulation and grades in elementary and high school. *British Journal of Educational Psychology.* doi:10.1111/bjep.12315

Maladaptive Perfectionism

One of the basic rules of the universe is that nothing is perfect. Perfection simply doesn't exist.

—**Stephen Hawking**

Understanding the Psychology

Perfect is like a magical unicorn creature. It would be so dang lovely to stumble upon one of those. Most unfortunately, heading out to look for a unicorn is a fool's errand. So, too, is searching, waiting, and aiming for a perfect draft. The other day I saw a woman wearing a shirt referencing a rhinoceros as a chubby unicorn, and I thought to myself—*beautiful.* Rhinoceroses may not be iridescent shades of all the colors and glowing with glitter, but they are unquestionably real. And there's beauty in the real. Similarly, there's beauty in the words you *have* written. What you have written is the beautiful, and extremely real, rhinoceros. In this chapter, you will learn how to embrace that chubby unicorn and send it out for review. But first, let's focus our attention on the magical unicorn creature of our imaginations—the idea of *perfect.*

What would perfect writing even look like? The perfect word? Sentence or section? Draft? Maybe perfect writing earns perfect praise in the feedback that you receive. Or, perhaps perfect means you could finally feel proud of your work. Many psychologists who study perfectionism differentiate people into three overarching categories: adaptive perfectionists, maladaptive perfectionists, and nonperfectionists (Moate et al., 2019; Ashby et al., 2012; Parker, 1997). Adaptive perfectionists are characterized by balancing the high personal standards they set and maintain with self-acceptance when they fall short of meeting their high standards. Similarly, maladaptive perfectionists also strive for high personal standards. What distinguishes maladaptive perfectionists from adaptive perfectionists is their tendency to be self-critical when they are unable to meet their high standards. Then we have nonperfectionists. Nonperfectionists do not burden themselves with the pressures of high standards. We're not going to spend too much time thinking about nonperfectionists in this chapter because—for better or worse—low standards are not a luxury academics can afford.

As you might have predicted, findings from several studies link positive outcomes with adaptive perfectionism and negative outcomes with maladaptive perfectionism. Adaptive perfectionists are often more satisfied with life (Rice & Ashby, 2007), hopeful (Ashby et al., 2011), and creative (Wigert et al., 2012) than their maladaptive perfectionist peers. Research suggests that those with maladaptive perfectionism also experience poor emotional well-being (Gnilka et al., 2012), heightened levels of stress (Ashby et al., 2012), and increased vulnerability to burnout (Stoeber & Rennert, 2008). In a recent study of faculty members, Moate et al. (2016) found that compared with adaptive perfectionists and nonperfectionists, maladaptive perfectionists had significantly higher levels of perceived stress, work-related burnout, personal burnout, and student-related burnout.[1] In a similar study with doctoral students, the same researchers found that adaptive perfectionists had lower levels of perceived stress and negative emotions and higher levels of positive emotions and general life satisfaction than maladaptive perfectionist students (Moate et al., 2019).

Perfectionism may be particularly counterproductive for academic writers. For example, in one study with men and womxn professors from all ranks, Sherry et al. (2010) found that those with a strong perfection-demanding orientation were less likely to submit manuscripts for publication and publish in high-impact journals. How is it that perfectionistic tendencies stifle our productivity and overall success? What is it that makes so many of us compulsively strive for perfection? The following sections dig into the heart of *maladaptive perfectionism*: perceived high standards set by others, unreasonable personal standards, overly critical self-evaluations, and fear of failure.

---

[1] That's a lot of burnout. Who knew there were so many types?!

Perceived Ridic Standards

Academics are typically high achievers. How did they get this way? Some likely had parents who were disappointed with anything less than perfect A's from preschool to college. Others were shaped by intimidating teachers who both prized and demanded brilliance. However they got here, these cute, sometimes neurotic, nerdlets then eventually found themselves in academia, surrounded by other high achievers and a culture that treasures high standards like Gollum treasures the One Ring.[2]

We need people and projects that challenge us. One of the fundamental aspects of academia is to do things that are difficult and study things that others haven't. However, the seemingly constant cycles of criticism, scrutiny, and rejection are the details that shape our perceptions of *what's expected*. We then sometimes turn into guessing basket cases in search of perfect.[3] This search of perfect can leave us either overdriven or paralyzed. Sounds familiar? That's when we have to say *Not today, Satan. Not today.* We're searching for a mystical creature that does not exist.

Your vision of perfect might be a note from an editor from a top journal saying that your article is accepted without revision. Or perhaps perfect means that your supervisor has only delightful praise to offer about your draft. It is not healthy, reasonable, or expected that you or your work be perfect. For reals. *Sure*, you might be thinking—*perfect actually is what is expected of me.* If these are your thoughts, then not only do you need to work on your own personal expectations of success, but you also have some work to do with the people for or with whom you're working.

Sometimes we find ourselves in situations with people who have power over us and our well-being, like advisers, supervisors, or department chairs, who actually seem to expect us to be perfect—or it at least feels that way. I won't take that away from you. I've been in that situation where I felt like the expectation for my manuscript or grant proposal had to be perfect or it wouldn't get accepted, published, funded, favorably reviewed, or otherwise. Those fears are not always all that far-fetched. However, if you strive for perfection, then you will drive yourself batty.[4] Period. The next sections will help you manage the conversation that you have with yourself about perfection. But before we get there, let's think about the direct

---

[2] *Imagines professor stroking a performance rubric while rocking and chanting, "My precious"*

[3] Where is that unicorn, anyway?

[4] Recall your emotional well-being when you made the manuscript folder titled "finalFINAL_Actuallyforrealfinal."

conversations that you need to have with others about expectations, standards, your progress, and success.

We're going to call these conversations #ExpectationManagement.[5] Have an intentional, explicit conversation with your adviser, supervisor, or department chair to set clear and specific expectations for your work. During this discussion, ask for exemplar works that you can model your own work after. Also, ask loads of questions. For example, you might ask *what types of mistakes do people make while they're writing a [type of manuscript/grant proposal/etc.]*? Or *what expectations do you have when you work with students/faculty? How do you typically handle the mistakes they make along the way? What advice might you give me for learning/working with you?* When we are clear with ourselves and others about the specific standards that are expected, we are then able to see precisely how high the bar is that we need to reach. After all, we're only able to reach the bar when we have a strategy for jumping that high. So, if during or after these conversations you realize that you need strategies to help you succeed, then make time for these discussions as well.

I'm not promising that these conversations will be easy. However, they don't have to be scary. One way to start the discussion in the right direction is to ask for the meeting with an email that illustrates that you care about your learning, progress, and success, and how you would like to ask a few questions to help you be as strategic as possible in that learning.

Chickity-Check Yo'Self Before You Wreck Yo'Self

'Cause perfectionism is bad for your health. Although those are not the *exact* lyrics to the song, I'm pretty sure Ice Cube would want you to check your perfectionistic ways. So do I.

Nearly every single definition of perfectionism includes the criterion, "unreasonably high standards." Let's think about standards for a hot second. Everyone has standards. It's just that some of us get a little carried away. Take for instance that one friend we all have—the one who wants to be in a relationship but has impossibly high standards for dating. This is the friend who refuses to date anyone who isn't vegan, is too tall or too short, is too outdoorsy, is gluten intolerant, has eyes that are too close together or too far apart, texts too much or too little,

---

[5] One of my former students, the brilliant Dr. Kim McKnight, taught me about the power of managing expectations.

> **Figure 5.1   Selected List of Wildly Unreasonable Writing Goals I've Set for My Writing**
>
> ### To Do
>
> 1. *Finish that manuscript this afternoon.*
> 2. *Write 10,000 words tomorrow.*
> 3. *Spend 12 hours writing. Every day this week. Without breaks.*

and smells like dryer sheets. This also happens to be the friend who is surprised they're alone. Similar to how our friend's absurd standards get in the way of them finding a unicorn to date, our own redic work standards can sabotage our productivity.

Research shows that doctoral writers often "set idealistic and unreachable goals for themselves" (Badenhorst, 2010). The tendency to set unreachable standards/goals doesn't magically disappear after grad school. It somehow seems to follow many of us throughout our careers. Worse, many perfectionists ratchet up the pressure over time. One study found that when perfectionists successfully met their standards, they then reevaluated those standards as insufficiently demanding (*After all, it didn't kill me, did it?!*), leading them to choose even more difficult standards for future tasks (Kobori et al., 2009).

I know I'm personally guilty of setting and trying to maintain impossible standards. Figure 5.1 shows a list of some of the wildly unrealistic goals I've set for my own writing. Blink twice if anything on this list has also held you hostage. Instead of motivating me, these outrageous standards usually lead me to either bury myself under no fewer than seven weighted blankets or watch a mind-numbing marathon of trash television on my comfy couch. Other times when I set out to work on my redic goals, I find that I have this remarkable ability to find things that absolutely need to be done that very minute. I'm like, *BRB, I need to go talk to some food. And clean the house. And make that dentist appointment. And* . . . altogether ignoring my work. When my ridiculous standards don't lead me to hibernate in a cave of my own dread or craft 18 creative excuses for not writing, I fixate on meeting my impractical goals by any means necessary. Waking to work long before the birds are up, carrying on until the wee hours of the night, and rarely stopping for trivial things like food or human interaction, my fixation resembles demonic possession.[6] In the end, no matter which of the unhealthy responses I choose, I find myself swaying from the top of the *bananas* tree.

The tippy top of the bananas tree is a very distressing place to be. One thing that helps me shimmy down is plainly identifying an attainable standard. As we discussed in Chapter 3 [Writing Stress and Anxiety], the goals we set for each of our writing sessions should be clear, proximal, measurable, and *actually* realistic for the amount of time we've set aside for writing. Not only does keeping my standards in check help me to avoid continuous disappointment, but it also helps me quiet the internal noise of guilt and despair that seems to creep into my writing process. Take the following for example—if I have an hour to write, I might set the goal of drafting 400 words. Then, if after an hour I find that I wrote 500 words, I'm feeling pretty fine! However, if I would have set my goal for 800 words and wrote the same 500 words, it's likely that I would have been really discouraged and found myself halfway up the bananas tree. My progress didn't change across the two examples. The only things to change were my goals and my resultant emotional reaction at the end of the hour. Realistic goals keep our eyes on progress and our motivation higher.

Shove Critical Cathy in the Closet

Perfectionism isn't only about unreasonably high and rigid standards; it's also about the overly critical evaluations of ourselves when those standards are not met. I call my fault-finding voice *Critical Cathy.* Before we are able to shove Critical Cathy into the closet, we must first be aware that the fool is in our heads and why she's there.

When you notice that your thoughts have turned meaner than Reviewer 2, you can start to consider where those thoughts come from or why they're there. Ask yourself *what is it about what I'm working on or how I'm working on it that might have spurred this self-attack? Why am I feeling such hostility? Are there other places in my life where my inner voice is/was so critical? What roles are my critical thoughts playing? How are these harsh thoughts actually serving me?* Perhaps your critical inner voice regularly tells you that your work isn't good enough and those thoughts might stem from several experiences with harsh feedback. After reflecting on why you might have those automatic thoughts, you have to decide how attached you want to be to your negative beliefs.

---

[6] Complete with wide eyes, sleep-deprivation, and mood swings, but thankfully without the 360-degree head spinning or projectile vomit.

There is a Cherokee legend (First People, n.d.) about an old man who says to his grandson, "A fight between two wolves is going on inside me. One wolf is evil—he is anger, envy, sorrow, regret, greed, arrogance, self-pity, guilt, resentment, inferiority, lies, false pride, superiority, and ego. The other wolf is good—he is joy, peace, love, hope, serenity, humility, kindness, benevolence, empathy, generosity, truth, compassion, and faith." When asked which wolf will win the fight, the old man replies, "The one I feed." The first wolf is definitely Critical Cathy—and she can be rather vociferous. We'll call the second wolf *Positive Patricia*. The voice of our Positive Patricia is sometimes drowned out by the rather loud and persistent voice of our Critical Cathy. We need to choose which of the two we're going to feed into.

To amplify Positive Patricia and head off Critical Cathy before she starts, begin in the right frame of mind by writing a counter statement on a sticky note (e.g., *LIES! My work IS good enough!*). Then keep this note in an obvious place for you to see while you write. For more on self-compassion, check out Chapter 9 [The Importance of Wellness and Self-Care].

Atelophobia

On today's episode of things that scare me, we're going to meet Atelophobia, or the fear of not doing something right or the fear of not being good enough (Greek word *atelo* meaning imperfection and *phobia* meaning fear). When we make a mistake in our writing it sometimes feels very public, and publicly failing can feel all things *horriful* (horrifying + awful). The other day while walking on the street, I totally biffed it after not noticing a sly patch of ice. What did I do? Well, I stood up and nonchalantly acted like it never happened, of course . . . because at that moment, I so very much wished that it hadn't happened. Physically, I was fine, but emotionally? Not so much. It was terribly upsetting. This falling event didn't happen in the privacy of my own driveway—or even my own neighborhood. My time to fall was right there on the sidewalk, outside my office, surrounded by So. Many. People. Ugh—embarrassing. If you live in a place where the temperature dips well below freezing, then chances are you, too, have fallen while trying to walk on ice. It's rather common. Similarly, making mistakes in our writing is pretty common. But those mistakes can feel like falling in public. Sometimes, the fear of making those mistakes can be crippling. Shame is often at the heart of our fears of failure. Imagining the deep shame we will feel if we make a mistake or disappoint others in our writing can make some avoid writing altogether. However, it's not as if people vow to never walk again after they slip in public, so why would you do the same with your writing?

Box 5.1 Evidence Checklist: Fear of Failure

You may be afraid of failure if:

☐ You worry about what others will think about your writing.

☐ You have a tremendously negative emotional response at the thought of your writing not being good enough.

☐ You steer clear of situations where others can judge your writing.

☐ You're vigilant about catching your own mistakes . . . before anyone else can.

☐ You'd rather not write at all than write something not great.

☐ Critical feedback in your writing makes you worry that you're not cut out for the future you planned.

☐ You worry that anything less than great writing will disappoint others.

☐ Receiving critical feedback makes you worry about how smart or capable you are.

☐ You get last-minute headaches, stomach pains, or other physical symptoms before deadlines.

If the list of evidence in Box 5.1 makes you feel all too seen, there are things you can do to overcome the fear blocking your writing success. The first and most important step is to own the fear. Accepting fear is critical before you are able to then discuss it with people you trust. In these conversations with others, you might get the reassurance and empathy you need to move forward. Next, it's essential to focus on manageable tasks that you can control. Although you can't control others' beliefs and feedback, the #ExpectationManagement conversation mentioned earlier in this chapter might give you ideas on where you can and should focus your attention and effort. Finally, define the failure line—literally write it down. What would failure *truly* look like? Then triple-check (and revise as necessary) to ensure that the failure line that you've set is actually healthy.

TL;DR Summary

- For the readers in the back, perfect writing is fantasy. Fantasies are OK, as long as you remember they're not real.

- The combination of both positive and negative dimensions make maladaptive perfectionism a sneaky bugger, because it's not always easy to discern between the positive and negative aspects.

- Both adaptive and maladaptive perfectionists focus on personally high standards, but only maladaptive perfectionists are overly self-critical when they fall short of achieving their goals.

- Maladaptive perfectionism has been linked with poor emotional well-being, heightened levels of stress, and burnout. Studies also show that maladaptive perfectionists publish less.

- Traits of maladaptive perfectionism include perceived high standards expected by others, personally set unreasonably high standards, overly critical self-evaluations, and fear of failure.

Essential Strategies for Productive (and Sane) Writing

If/when you notice your perfectionism getting in the way of your writing productivity, there are ways to keep your mind in check. Read the following sections and choose one or two strategies to begin.

Put Your Cocktail Dress and Bowtie Away. It's Just a Draft

So often, panic sets in for me when I stare at the blinking cursor on a blank page of my computer screen. *What am I doing?* I think to myself. *I have zero of the ideas. Zero. I really have no idea what I'm doing.*[7] And then it's like the cursor is nodding right along with me, agreeing that I truly don't have any ideas.

It's times like these when I look around and notice all the "reasons" I'm struggling. Like, *Obviously! I hate writing on the computer! I write better using a pen and paper—my bamboo aromatherapy pen infused with refreshing*

---

[7] Shout-out to my pal, Imposter Syndrome!

peppermint to clear my mind, to be exact. Or, of course, this place just doesn't have the right vibe for me to write. It's sucking my mojo dry. I need to move. Or, I don't have enough time to write right now. I'll get to it later. Whatever "reason" I come up with is actually an excuse to help relieve my guilt for not writing at that very moment. These excuses turn writing into a special event. Friends, writing is not an event—not when our degrees/jobs depend on us being writers, at least. Sure, we all have ideal standards for how, when, and where we write, but having the best equipment in the dreamiest of settings is not usually our ForReal.com. In real life, we have to make the most out of imperfect and tolerate the nonideal like writing in a windowless office cube or with boring dollar-store pens.

To build a strong writing habit, you should write every single day, and lowering your standards will help you realize that you really can write anywhere. Where do you have 15 minutes in your day? Everyone has 15 minutes.[8] Maybe use the 15 minutes on your commute to work to dictate your ideas for the introduction of your manuscript. Or spend the 15 minutes it takes you to walk from your car to your office with your headphones on, listening to the draft of the section you wrote yesterday (for more on dictating and listening to your writing, see Chapter 3 [Writing Stress and Anxiety]). They may not be the most ideal 15 minutes, but in those 15 minutes you made progress (remember that any task you do that advances your writing project counts as writing!). Recall from the last chapter [Writing Self-efficacy], even small moments of success can build our writing efficacy beliefs. Each day that you write for even a few minutes builds your writing practice. And keep in mind—*there's a reason we call a practice.*

The Mess Is Where We Begin

There's this amaaaazing children's book, *Beautiful Oops*, by Barney Saltz-berg (2010), and everything about it really is beautiful. Throughout its pages, the book shows readers how to creatively reframe mistakes into art. An accidentally torn page is turned into alligator mouth and a paint spill into a goofy animal. In a more grown-up book (and one of my faves on writing), *Bird by Bird*, Anne Lamott (2007) also focuses on the power of messes. She writes that whereas perfectionism is a "mean, frozen form of idealism," messes can be a "true friend" (p. 32). She then reminds us that our messes help us to figure out our identity and purpose. It might not yet be pretty, but there's value in the mess of our first drafts—the mess is where we begin. Lamott calls this mess a sh*tty first draft, the draft where we get out all of our thoughts, feels, and

---

[8] Even you, Janice.

ideas. This is the draft where you write with great abandon. With a devil-may-care attitude, write every word that comes to mind. Write without judgment because this is a draft that no one else is going to see. This is your beautiful, chubby rhinoceros unicorn. Keep it in a file that only you can see. The sentences you see in this file are the teeny tiny little idea babies that will help you think along the way—the ones that might come to life in the next draft.

Defining #GoodEnough

There's this saying often heard in many grad programs: *The best dissertation is a done dissertation.* Though no doubt trite, there is a lot of truth in this wisdom nugget. Your dissertation is not your magnum opus. I remember hearing those words and feeling like, *What?! This is the biggest thing I've ever done and it feels like the biggest thing I'll ever do!* But it wasn't.[9] Similarly, when I'm writing a manuscript for a prestigious journal, it feels really important, like this actually *could* be my magnum opus—and that tends to freak me out a bit. When we strive for the very best, we lose focus on good enough. Good enough is not only healthy, it can be satisfying, too. And, more times than not, good enough passes thesis defenses, and good enough gets published (eventually). Every writing session, define what will be #GoodEnough for that day.

Burn It

The next time you're feeling overwhelmed with your writing, close your eyes and sit quietly. Listen closely to your thoughts. Who do you hear—*Critical Cathy* or *Positive Patricia*? If you're stuck, then chances are that you hear that jerk, Critical Cathy. What is she saying? That you don't know what you're doing? That your ideas are embarrassing? On a sheet of paper, write down the things that you hear. Then rip each statement into its own, small shred of paper. Choose the statements that you're ready to release and prepare to burn that shish.[10] When you're ready, take a few deep, relaxing breaths. Light each piece of paper on fire, watch it blaze, and let that mother go.

---

[9] Looking back, thank heavens it wasn't the biggest or best thing I ever did—my dissertation was only slightly better than my absolutely terrible master's thesis.

[10] You'll need matches or a lighter, a safe, burn-friendly surface (e.g., a metal or glass bowl, fireplace, etc.), and an open space like a backyard or garden. You probably already know that . . . because you have/are working on an advanced degree. Safety first!

NEXT STEPS

- Explicitly ask others about their expectations for your work to set the record straight (#ExpectationManagement).

- Standards for excellence are important, but there's a difference between your best and perfect. Don't be a goal digger. Keep your standards in check by setting goals that are clear, proximal, measurable, and actually realistic for the amount of time you've set aside for writing.

- Owning and talking about your fear of failure are the first steps to stopping it from blocking your writing success.

- Write down what will define failure in your work or writing. Evaluate your definition to ensure it's a healthy standard.

- When you're unable to write, track the obstacles that stood in your way. Explore the patterns that emerge and define the steps you can take to make more space for writing.

- Begin to build a writing habit by writing for 15 minutes every single day. Be creative about where you find those 15 minutes!

- Accept and embrace the messiness of your first draft. Let it be jagged rough.

- At the beginning of each writing session, define what will count as #GoodEnough for that day and work toward that, not perfection.

- Pay close attention to your inner voice to recognize—and stop—critical self-statements. Write each critical statement on a slip of paper. Take them to the fire pit and, when you're ready to let them go, light 'em up.

EXTRA RESOURCES

Antony, M. M., & Swinson, R. P. (2009). *When perfect isn't good enough: Strategies for coping with perfectionism*. New Harbinger Publications.

Brown, B. (2010). *The gifts of imperfection: Let go of who you think you're supposed to be and embrace who you are*. Hazelden Publishing.

Lamoot, A. (2007). *Bird by bird: Some instructions on writing and life*. Anchor.

Saujani, R. (2019). *Brave, not perfect: Fear less, fail more, and live bolder.* Currency Press.

Somov, P. G. (2010). *Present perfect: A mindfulness approach to letting go of perfectionism and the need for control.* New Harbinger Publications.

HUMOR BREAK

Quiz: Perfectionism: Which *Friends* Character Are You?[11]

Complete the following quiz to reveal your level of perfectionism.

1. After finishing a draft, you focus on:

   A. Punctuation. I can spend hours looking at commas and semicolons, and deciding if I put them in the correct place.
   B. Clarity. I torture myself over not just identifying gaps in the literature but explaining why each gap is important to address.
   C. Your amazing writing. You are incredibly talented.

2. Which of the following most accurately describes you?

   A. I can't decide between thoroughness and wordiness. Do I explain more and risk being too wordy to follow, or be succinct and risk things being unclear to readers? Is *thwordy* a thing??
   B. Correctly formatting references haunts my sleep.
   C. When I write, I am totally drunk with power.

3. Which of the following sounds most like you?

   A. "Are there two spaces or one?! It's one! Right?? Or is it two??"
   B. "Is everything connected? Does each section flow well?"
   C. "Plan? I don't even have a pla-."

---

[11] Disclaimer: This quiz is ridiculous and in no way scientifically accurate.

MOSTLY A's: Monica: *"And remember, if I'm harsh with you, it's only because you're doing it wrong."* Whether you like it or not, perfectionism is totally your jam. Every bit of your writing must be organized, and every detail must be meticulously in its place. You use your label maker to label the folders of your writing projects, you make lists of the lists you need to make, and harsh criticism makes you eat sheet cake. Most of this stems from your uncontrollable need to please people.

MOSTLY B's: Ross: *"By the way, Y-O-U-apostrophe-R-E means YOU ARE. Y-O-U-R means YOUR!"* So you might be a touch of a perfectionist. You're the only one out of your friends with a PhD so you take it upon yourself to help everyone with their grammar and spelling. It makes your ears bleed to hear "whom" and "who" misused. Luckily, you still have other nerdy friends in PhD-Land.

MOSTLY C's: Phoebe: *"Oh my God, I sound amazing!"* Perfectionism rarely gets you down. You only mind a little bit when Monica hates the songs you write. After all, you did write the smash hit "Smelly Cat." Similar to your running style, you don't care who sees what you've written, no matter how quirky it might seem to others.

Activity: Perfectionism Voodoo Doll

This voodoo doll will repel the negative energies of your perfectionism. After cutting out the doll, simply use thumbtacks or draw pins to prick your perfectionistic tendencies that need repelling. Skip to the perforated pages at the end of the book for a voodoo doll that's ready for your cork board.

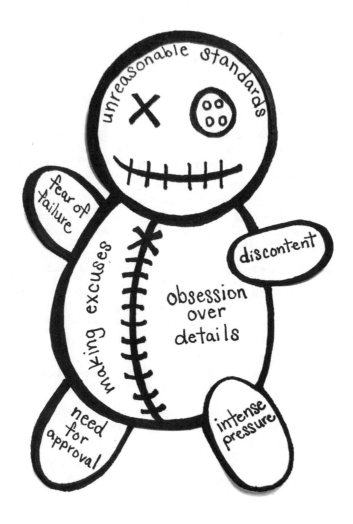

References

Ashby, J. S., Dickinson, W. L., Gnilka, P. B., & Noble, C. L. (2011). Hope as a mediator and moderator of multidimensional perfectionism and depression in middle school students. *Journal of Counseling & Development, 89*(2), 131–139. doi:10.1002/j.1556-6678.2011.tb00070.x

Ashby, J. S., Noble, C. L., & Gnilka, P. B. (2012). Multidimensional perfectionism, depression, and satisfaction with life: Differences among perfectionists and tests of a stress-mediation model. *Journal of College Counseling, 15*(2), 130–143. doi:10.1002/j.2161-1882.2012.00011.x

Badenhorst, C. (2010). *Productive writing: Becoming a prolific academic writer.*Van Schaik Publishers.

First People. (n.d.). Two wolves: a Cherokee legend. https://www.firstpeople.us/FP-Html-Legends/TwoWolves-Cherokee.html

Gnilka, P. B., Ashby, J. S., & Noble, C. M. (2012). Multidimensional perfectionism and anxiety: Differences among individuals with perfectionism and tests of a coping-mediation model. *Journal of Counseling & Development, 90*(4), 427–436. doi:10.1002/j.1556-6676.2012.00054.x

Kobori, O., Hayakawa, M., & Tanno, Y. (2009). Do perfectionists raise their standards after success? An experimental examination of the revaluation of standard setting in perfectionism. *Journal of Behavior Therapy and Experimental Psychiatry, 40*(4), 515–521. doi:10.1016/j.jbtep.2009.07.003

Lamott, A. (2007). *Bird by bird: Some instructions on writing and life.* Anchor Books.

Moate, R. M., Gnilka, P. B., West, E. M., & Bruns, K. L. (2016). Stress and burnout among counselor educators: Differences between adaptive perfectionists, maladaptive perfectionists, and nonperfectionists. *Journal of Counseling and Development, 94*(2), 161–171. doi:10.1002/jcad.12073

Moate, R. M., Gnilka, P. B., West, E. M., & Rice, K. G. (2019). Doctoral student perfectionism and emotional well-being. *Measurement and Evaluation in Counseling and Development, 52*(3), 145–155. doi:10.1080/07481756.2018.1547619

Parker, W. D. (1997). An empirical typology of perfectionism in academically talented children. *American Educational Research Journal, 34*(3), 545–562. doi:10.3102/00028312034003545

Rice, K. G., & Ashby, J. S. (2007). An efficient method for classifying perfectionists. *Journal of Counseling Psychology, 54*(1), 72–85. doi:10.1037/0022-0167.54.1.72

Saltzberg, B. (2010). *Beautiful oops!* Workman Publishing.

Sherry, S. B., Hewitt, P. L., Sherry, D. L., Flett, G. L., & Graham, A. R. (2010). Perfectionism dimensions and research productivity in psychology professors: Implications for understanding the (mal)adaptiveness of perfectionism. *Canadian Journal of*

Behavioural Science/Revue canadienne des sciences du comportement, 42(4), 273–283. doi:10.1037/a0020466

Stoeber, J., & Rennert, D. (2008). Perfectionism in school teachers: Relations with stress appraisals, coping styles, and burnout. *Anxiety, Stress, and Coping, 21*(1), 37–53. doi:10.1080/10615800701742461

Wigert, B., Reiter-Palmon, R., Kaufman, J. C., & Silvia, P. J. (2012). Perfectionism: The good, the bad, and the creative. *Journal of Research in Personality, 46*(6), 775–779. doi:10.1016/j.jrp.2012.08.007

6

Autonomy in Our Work and Writing

The only person you're in charge of is you.

—My mom, often

Understanding the Psychology

A large part of the human adventure is finding our purpose on this planet. As professional nerds, much of our adventure is dedicated to doing the work we think the world needs. One of our first opportunities to do this work comes with our passport to DissertationLand (DLand[1]). In DLand, students develop a sense of themselves as expert scholars in a particular field, and while there, the dissertation serves not only as evidence that students know the important work that the field needs, but also as evidence that they are able to do the work that needs to be done. Traveling through the mysterious DLand requires the navigation assistance of a knowledgeable guide; however, much of students' time and effort while there requires independence and autonomy. And, on the other side of DLand, some students find themselves as new faculty members or researchers within academia where independence and autonomy are both critically valued and critically important.

For students and new faculty alike, this autonomy can be empowering, as it's an opportunity to prove ourselves and contribute to our communities and fields. Sometimes, however, autonomy and independence can freak a nerd out (*Where do I begin? What work would make a difference? How does one ever decide?!*). Yet other times, it can seem like we really don't have much autonomy at all, and lacking a sense of control can rain on our passion parade.

---

[1] Not to be confused with Disneyland. Disneyland is very, *very* different from DissertationLand.

In the following sections, we'll dig into autonomy and why it's central for our scholarship, research, and writing. We'll also explore the autonomy files of "too much" and "too little," and how to get the right levels of control and independence you need to make progress in your academic work.

The Ins and Outs of Autonomy

One of our basic psychological needs is autonomy, or "the necessity of experiencing a sense of choice, willingness, and volition as one behaves" (Deci et al., 2013, p. 113). According to self-determination theory (Deci & Ryan, 2008), other basic psychological needs include competence (see Chapter 4 [Writing Self-efficacy]) and relatedness (see Chapter 8 [Finding Social Support for Writing]). When our needs are satisfied, we are happier, more productive humans (Deci & Ryan, 2012). One meta-analytic review of employee attitudes showed that autonomy related negatively to strain and burnout and positively to positive affect, engagement, and general well-being (Van den Broeck et al., 2016). And autonomy seems to matter for happiness everywhere. In another meta-analysis of 36 samples across the United States and all East Asian countries, Yu et al., (2018) found that autonomy need satisfaction universally related to subjective well-being across both Eastern and Western cultures.

The power of autonomy is clear in academia for both graduate students and faculty. In a recent study, Litalien et al. (2015) found that students who felt their goals and behaviors were of their own volition and choice were more likely to feel satisfied with their studies, program, and university and experience positive emotions and lower test anxiety; were more productive and less likely to experience problems in their thesis work; and were less likely to drop out of their programs than participants who were motivated by internal pressures to avoid guilt and shame. Similarly, findings from studies with faculty members show that autonomy relates to motivation, sense of research success, and overall productivity (Stupnisky et al., 2017; Walker & Fenton, 2013). In a study of minority faculty, Lechuga (2012) found that most were motivated to engage in research when they perceived the work to be meaningful.

What is it that leads us to feel more independent? Though our sense of control is internal, like most other things in life, our environment plays a fundamental role in how supported we feel in our efforts to be autonomous. To feel optimal control over our work, we need both support and resources. Use the checklist in Box 6.1 to determine how

Box 6.1 Evidence Checklist: Autonomy-Supportive Environments for Research and Writing

☐ You feel like you have a choice in your research topic, design, and methodology.

☐ Others encourage you to come up with ideas for your work.

☐ There is flexibility if you change your mind about topic or methodology.

☐ Others support your initiative.

☐ You have a say about when and where you work.

☐ Others take time to listen to your ideas.

☐ You feel like you have a choice in how you write and where you publish.

☐ There is flexibility for how you handle challenges that arise.

☐ Others provide feedback in a supportive, nonjudgmental way.

☐ You have flexibility over your time line for completion for your work.

much your environment sets you up to be autonomous in your scholarship and writing.

Too Much of a Good Thing?

Some will look at the list in the box and be able to check off several of the items, noticing that they have quite a bit of autonomy over their work. However, too much choice can feel overwhelming. For instance, raise your hand if you've stood in an aisle at the grocery store for far too long considering the dizzying array of options for whitening toothpaste or hot sauce.[2] Research suggests choice overload is a real thing (Chernev et al., 2015). In a classic experiment (Iyengar & Lepper, 2000), shoppers

---

[2] Thoughts while grocery shopping: *Which one of these toothpastes will make my teeth actually sparkle? What's the proof? Are these ingredients natural? What's the difference between "max white," "advanced white,'" "noticeably white," and "optic white?" Now how are there 500 hot sauces to choose from?! How do I choose between "Goddess of Fire" and "Mo Hotta, Mo Betta"? I'm going to have to pass on "Dave's Ultimate Insanity Hot Sauce'" and "Blair's Original Death Sauce." Sorry, Dave and Blair.*

in different conditions were shown either an extensive assortment of 24 or a modest display of six exotic flavors of jam. Findings showed that more people stopped by the booth with more options,[3] but it was the customers with more limited options who were more likely to end up purchasing a jar of fancy jam. Similar to our experiences with toothpaste, hot sauce, and jam in the grocery store, we can feel paralyzed with the number of choices we have in our research and writing. Perhaps your graduate adviser tells you that your dissertation can be on anything you want—well, probably not anything you want, but you feel like choosing the topic is largely up to you. Or, perhaps you're a new faculty member with heaps of academic freedom. Sometimes when the world is our oyster, we wonder if we might be a wee bit allergic to shellfish. Feelings of being overwhelmed can make us want to postpone making decisions. After all, choosing the "right" research topic can seem really important. When it comes to being besieged with choice, it's normal to look to others for guidance. The trick is finding the right guide to help you make sense of all your options. Seek out mentors who not only honor your autonomy but also invest in conversations to help you make thoughtful decisions about your work.

Too Little of a Good Thing?

If looking at the checklist in Box 6.1 makes you feel more controlled than the variables in your statistical model, then it's likely that you're not feeling terribly motivated about your work. Sometimes it seems like our work is out of our hands, and that can suck the interest out of a project. You might feel pressure to study a topic that has the support of your research mentor or senior colleagues, because these are the individuals seemingly at the gates of your graduation or tenure (Brodin, 2016). In fact, some dissertation chairs make the expectation clear that their students' thesis topics relate to their work, which might not be in line with the research interests of the students.

Academics may also feel as if the direction of their work is determined by the work they've already done. When I go to restaurants, I'm the person who classically orders the exact same thing every time. Sure, I always choose something that's reliable and safe, but I'm often jealous of my adventurous friends who choose the extra-special special that turns out to be actually quite special. Similarly, I have felt constrained to continue the line of work even when my interest waned or wandered, eyeing a

---

[3] Um, 24 different types of jam? Who could pass up such an impressive display?!

sparkly, new research topic, all of sudden hungry for something different. If, for whatever reason, you're feeling constrained to work on research that does not interest you, then it's time to call a meeting with yourself to figure out what it is you want to be working on, why you want to work on it, and how you're going to make doing that work a possibility. Then you might need meet with your supervisor or mentor to get feedback on your plan.

Newbie Struggles

When we're new to a field or a line of research or scholarship, it makes sense for our independence to be somewhat limited as we learn. This learning typically requires the assistance and guidance of others, and people react differently to the necessary requirement of support. While some feel content, others feel torn by their need for help and their need to feel independently competent (Gardner, 2008). For example, I recently had a doctoral student who was equally annoyed and apologetic about the help she needed from me with her dissertation. As the chair of her committee, I remember kindly telling her that it was a tad arrogant for her to think that she would be able to complete her dissertation without any help. *Really? You thought you could just roll up in here and do this on your own? Well, then don't mind me, I'll just be over here in my hammock sipping on this here refreshing beverage.* Please. Everybody who's doing anything worth doing needs a village to make it as successful as possible. This is true in PhD Land and beyond. Whether you're a graduate student, early career scholar, or a seasoned faculty member, you need support. For more on building a village, see Chapter 8 [Finding Social Support for Writing]. Look for mentors and peers who empower your ideas and voice. Also keep your eye out for collaborative opportunities that allow you to gain autonomy as you learn the ropes. And, if you find yourself thinking that you need to do all the things all by yourself, consider reflecting on why that might be and if those thoughts reflect what is or could be true. Might the work or the process be better or more efficient, or more enjoyable with the perspective of at least one other human?

TL;DR Summary

- Autonomy is one of our basic psychological needs and is defined as our sense of control, willingness, and volition over our behavior.

- We are much happier and more productive when we feel autonomous.

- As academics, our sense of autonomy relates to positive emotions, motivation, persistence, and success.

- Our environment plays a critical role in how autonomous we feel in our work and writing.

- Autonomy-supportive environments provide a safe place for you to voice your ideas and make flexible decisions about with whom, what, when, where, and how you work.

- Too much autonomy can feel overwhelming, but strong mentors can help you make thoughtful decisions.

- Too little autonomy can feel restrictive and demotivating and signals the need for change.

- It's normal for newbies to a field, line of research or scholarship, genre of writing, or research methodology to feel torn between their need for help and their need to feel independent and confident.

Essential Strategies for Productive (and Sane) Writing

Sometimes, our sense of autonomy over our work wavers. When this happens to you, you've got work to do to begin steering yourself toward meaningful projects with aspects that you can control. Choose one to two ideas from the following sections to get started.

Laser Focus

Remembering the real reasons why we write can keep us focused in the right direction. However, the word "should" can creep into our thoughts and conversations when it comes to our work—things we *should* do, *should* think about, *should* want, blah, blah, blah. Y'all, *don't should the bed. Shoulding* can take a

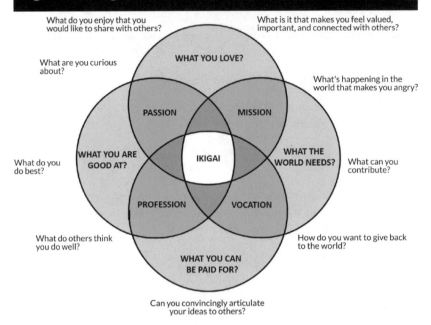

Figure 6.1 *Ikigai* Guide to Autonomous Work

What do you enjoy that you would like to share with others?

What is it that makes you feel valued, important, and connected with others?

What are you curious about?

WHAT YOU LOVE?

What's happening in the world that makes you angry?

PASSION

MISSION

What do you do best?

WHAT YOU ARE GOOD AT?

IKIGAI

WHAT THE WORLD NEEDS?

What can you contribute?

PROFESSION

VOCATION

What do others think you do well?

How do you want to give back to the world?

WHAT YOU CAN BE PAID FOR?

Can you convincingly articulate your ideas to others?

Adapted from http://theviewinside.me/what-is-your-ikigai/

toll on your emotional health. One study found that participants who more often felt like they should be doing something else other than the activity they were doing had lower well-being and life-satisfaction scores than participants who experienced fewer motivational conflicts (Grund et al, 2015).

The next time you find yourself *shoulding* about your work, consider: What is the work that you actually want to do? What's the itch you need to scratch?[4] The Japanese word *ikigai* roughly translates into "reason for being," and jazz musician and author Tim Tamashiro calls it a treasure map to finding your purpose. Comprising overlapping circles representing passions, gifts,[5] possibilities, and values, we can use *ikigai* to guide our academic efforts. Use the questions in Figure 6.1 to get a clearer sense of the authentically aligned work that can improve your autonomy. It's normal for your answers to these questions to change as you grow as a scholar. Keep a running list of your answers and the research and writing interests they spark. For now, your

---

[4] Literally. Ok, not literally, but seriously.

[5] The VIA Institute on Character (www.viacharacter.org) has a free survey that can help you discover your strengths.

answers give you a place to start doing work that's meaningful to you. But, don't get me wrong, this work might not be all rainbows and glitter. Meaningful work is difficult, and difficult is sometimes the opposite of glitter rainbows. Difficult can be uncomfortable and exhausting. But difficult work can be meaningful—and that's the key. Doing work you believe to be meaningful will help you feel fulfilled and can make the writing associated with that work much more enjoyable.

Define What's Yours

When our autonomy on a project is diminished, completing the writing that is necessary to get it out of our lives can feel dreadful. However, focusing on the components in your power can be motivating. Which pieces are in your jurisdiction? Use Figure 6.2 to first take inventory of what you do and don't control. Perhaps you don't have an opportunity to weigh in about the audience for your work, but your voice—and the way your voice shows up in your writing—is yours. And maybe your office is a windowless closet in the dungeon of the ivory tower. If this isn't your favorite place to be, then are you able to write in a different space? After inventorying aspects of your writing autonomy, find whatever gratitude you can muster for the components under your control and make an effort

Figure 6.2 Writing Autonomy Inventory	
Potential Autonomy Components	**Questions to Ask**
Who	For which audience are you writing? Do you have freedom to select the outlet? Also, with whom do you write? Are you able to write/work with the people you choose? Can you make more time with the humans you appreciate on the project? Are you able to write alone or with others working on a different project?
What	Do you have any sway over the topic? Is there a subtopic you might be able to spin-off of the project? Is there room to add anything to the project to make it more interesting or valuable for you?
When	Is there latitude for when you choose to work on the project? Are you able to write at the time that works best for you? Is there flexibility for how you prioritize your projects and other responsibilities?
Where	Do you have the opportunity to write wherever you'd like?
Why	Is there a way to find meaningfulness in your project? What skills are you learning? Who is the work benefiting?
How	Is there flexibility in how you write? Are you able to write according to your preferences (e.g. pen/paper, word processor, etc.)? Are you able to write with your authentic voice and style?

to keep your focus there. Remember from Chapter 4 [Writing Self-efficacy] that a little gratitude can go a long way. Then consider the areas where you would like more autonomy in your project or writing and make a plan for doing more of the work that you find rewarding.

Find Your Writing Mojo

In the last chapter [5; Maladaptive Perfectionism], we discussed how ideal settings are unnecessary to productive writing. This is 100% true, but it's also true that switching up your setting can bring you a sense of peace and help you get your groove back.[6] Whereas staying inside in the same location might squash our creativity and mood, nature-like surroundings can spark positive mood states and higher levels of cognitive arousal (Tyrväinen et al., 2014). In one study, participants experienced mood improvement by simply sitting outside for five minutes (Neill et al., 2019). Anecdotally, I personally attest to the truth in these findings and make it a habit to find enjoyable places to write. Sometimes I hightail it to my favorite local coffee shop that has a great window overlooking a cute, urban garden. Other times, I corral a couple colleagues to join me for a woodsy writing retreat in a shabby and cost-effective cabin at one of the nearby state parks. And, it doesn't happen often, but sometimes I splurge on a writing workcation[7] at the beach because that is where my spirit happens to live. I've found that even moving my writing space to my porch can give me the change of scenery necessary for boosting my productivity mojo.

Similar to how I like to shake things up and write in different locations, I like to work on my projects in different formats. For instance, sometimes I print out my draft and grab my favorite pen to mark it up. Other times, I take a step back and draw out my ideas with a concept map or sketches. To try this for yourself, consider the images that might represent your ideas. Then make a quick sketch on a sheet of paper or copy and paste electronic images of your ideas to a virtual document. How do the images help you see your ideas differently? How do the images relate to one another?

When all else fails, sometimes it helps to take a break and turn my data into a series of catterplots[8]—because data is most assuredly more enjoyable to both look at and write about when it is represented by hordes of cats. In the end, swapping out where or how you work might have a butterfly effect on your writing motivation and productivity.

---

[6] Please note that there is currently no empirical evidence to suggest that changing your place will also lead to a romantic rendezvous like it did in the movie *How Stella Got Her Groove Back*.

[7] Work + Vacation = Workcation

[8] For more information on catterplots, go to https://github.com/Gibbsdavidl/CatterPlots

NEXT STEPS

- Keep an eye out for the people who empower your ideas as well as supportive opportunities to work on those ideas.

- Truly meaningful work is a balance of our interests, strengths, possibilities, and values. Do some soul searching/thinking/journaling/ talking with others about the kinds of meaningful work that might be best for you. Keep in mind that pursuing such work is fulfilling, but often difficult.

- Potential areas of our work and writing autonomy include: who, what, when, where, why, and how. Assess the areas of your work that are under your control and focus your attention there.

- Switching up where or how you work can provide motivation and inspiration. Try writing in a new place (e.g., coffee shop, cabin, beach, etc.) or in a different format (e.g., concept map, images, dictation).

EXTRA RESOURCES

Pink, D. H. (2011). *Drive: The surprising truth about what motivates us*. Penguin.

Ryan, R. M., & Deci, E. L. (2000). Self-determination theory and the facilitation of intrinsic motivation, social development, and well-being. *American Psychologist, 55*(1), 68–78.

Schwartz, B. (2004). *The paradox of choice: Why more is less* (Vol. 6). HarperCollins.

van Schalkwyk, S. C., Murdoch-Eaton, D., Tekian, A., Van der Vleuten, C., & Cilliers, F. (2016). The supervisor's toolkit: A framework for doctoral supervision in health professions education: AMEE Guide No. 104. *Medical Teacher, 38*(5), 429–442.

Quiz: What's Chasing You in Your Dreams? What Your Dreams Reveal About Your Autonomy.[9]

Of the list below, choose the last thing you remember chasing you in your dreams. Then read the description to learn the prophecy of your dreams for your level of autonomy.

Scary Stranger: Someone or something unknown, dark, and threatening has control over your control. Level of autonomy: *Exceptionally Low.*

Spider or Some Other Terrifying Wild Animal: You feel pressured to work on others' projects and this makes you fighting mad. Level of autonomy: *Quite Low.*

Vampire or Zombie: It's been 84 long years since you've done work that actually interests you and it feels like death will never come. Level of autonomy: *Super Low.*

Very Large, Random Object(s): You are overwhelmed with the zillion choices you have to make on a daily basis and would like someone—anyone—to make even one decision for you. Level of autonomy: *Overpoweringly High.*

Golden Rays of Sunshine: Living your best life, you are content, curious, and open to possibilities. Level of autonomy: *Dreamily*[10] *High.*

---

[9] Disclaimer: This quiz is ridiculous and in no way scientifically accurate.
[10] See what I did there?

Activity: Things-You-Can-Control Coloring Page

Skip to the perforated pages at the end of the book and shade the images that you have control over.

how you spend
your time

the temperature
in your office

your computer

your writing

you (*hint: you're
already shaded!*)

where you work

saving your work

father time

your pen

your cat

your collaborators

rush-hour traffic

References

Brodin, E. M. (2016). Critical and creative thinking nexus: Learning experiences of doctoral students. *Studies in Higher Education, 41*(6), 971–989. doi:10.1080/03075079 .2014.943656

Chernev, A., Böckenholt, U., & Goodman, J. (2015). Choice overload: A conceptual review and meta-analysis. *Journal of Consumer Psychology, 25*(2), 333–358. doi:10.1016/j. jcps.2014.08.002

Deci, E. L., & Ryan, R. M. (2008). Facilitating optimal motivation and psychological well-being across life's domains. *Canadian Psychology/Psychologie canadienne, 49*(1), 14–23. doi:10.1037/0708-5591.49.1.14

Deci, E. L., & Ryan, R. M. (2012). *Motivation, personality, and development within embedded social contexts: An overview of self-determination theory.* In R. M. Ryan (Ed.), *The Oxford Handbook of human motivation* (pp. 85–107). Oxford University Press.

Deci, E. L., Ryan, R. M., & Guay, F. (2013). *Self-determination theory and actualization of human potential.* In D. McInerney, H. Marsh, R. Craven, & F. Guay (Eds.), *Theory driving research: New wave perspectives on self-processes and human development* (pp. 109–133). Information Age Press.

Gardner, S. K. (2008). "What's too much and what's too little?": The process of becoming an independent researcher in doctoral education. *The Journal of Higher Education, 79*(3), 326–350. doi:10.1080/00221546.2008.11772101

Grund, A., Grunschel, C., Bruhn, D., & Fries, S. (2015). Torn between want and should: An experience-sampling study on motivational conflict, well-being, self-control, and mindfulness. *Motivation and Emotion, 39*(4), 506–520. doi:10.1007/s11031-015-9476-z

Iyengar, S. S., & Lepper, M. R. (2000). When choice is demotivating: Can one desire too much of a good thing? *Journal of Personality and Social Psychology, 79*(6), 995–1006. doi:10.1037/0022-3514.79.6.995

Lechuga, V. M. (2012). Latino faculty in STEM disciplines: Motivation to engage in research activities. *Journal of Latinos and Education, 11*(2), 107–123. doi:10.1080 /15348431.2012.659564

Litalien, D., Guay, F., & Morin, A. J. S. (2015). Motivation for PhD studies: Scale development and validation. *Learning and Individual Differences, 41*, 1–13. doi:10.1016/j.lindif.2015.05.006

Neill, C., Gerard, J., & Arbuthnott, K. D. (2019). Nature contact and mood benefits: Contact duration and mood type. *The Journal of Positive Psychology, 14*(6), 756–767. doi:10.1080/1743 9760.2018.1557242

Stupnisky, R. H., Hall, N. C., Daniels, L. M., & Mensah, E. (2017). Testing a model of pretenure faculty members' teaching and research success: Motivation as a mediator of balance, expectations, and collegiality. *The Journal of Higher Education, 88*(3), 376–400. doi:1 0.1080/00221546.2016.1272317

Tyrväinen, L., Ojala, A., Korpela, K., Lanki, T., Tsunetsugu, Y., & Kagawa, T. (2014). The influence of urban green environments on stress relief measures: A field experiment. *Journal of Environmental Psychology, 38*, 1–9. doi:10.1016/j.jenvp.2013.12.005

Van den Broeck, A., Ferris, D. L., Chang, C.-H., & Rosen, C. C. (2016). A review of self-determination theory's basic psychological needs at work. *Journal of Management, 42*(5), 1195–1229. doi:10.1177/0149206316632058

Walker, G. J., & Fenton, L. (2013). Backgrounds of, and factors affecting, highly productive leisure researchers. *Journal of Leisure Research, 45*(4), 537–562. doi:10.18666/jlr-2013-v45-i4-3898

Yu, S., Levesque-Bristol, C., & Maeda, Y. (2018). General need for autonomy and subjective well-being: A meta-analysis of studies in the US and East Asia. *Journal of Happiness Studies, 19*(6), 1863–1882. doi:10.1007/s10902-017-9898-2

Embracing the Feedback Process[1]

I like criticism. It makes you strong.

—LeBron James

Understanding the Psychology

If liking criticism is how we need to feel to be stronger writers, then that might be a tough pill for some of us to swallow. At its best, criticism can identify challenging or unpleasant work for us to do to improve our writing; at its worst, criticism can break our hearts. So, sometimes, ignorance really might seem like bliss. In one psychological study of the human appetite for ignorance, students watched a fake educational film about a serious disease (Howell & Shepperd, 2013). While watching, students were unaware that the serious disease was actually fictitious. After the film, all study participants were given the opportunity to provide a cheek swab to assess their risk of developing the disease. While half of the group was told that if they ever developed the disease, then treatment would entail a two-week course of pills, the other half was told that treatment would involve taking the pills for the rest of their lives. The findings? Whereas over half of the two-week treatment participants agreed to the diagnostic cheek swab, fewer than a quarter of the pill-for-life group agreed to the swab. In this study, the pill-for-lifers would just rather not know the news, thank you very much. Like a diagnostic swab, honest criticism can be precisely the thing that identifies how we can make our work better—even great. And, in ways similar to medication, feedback—both praise and criticism—is effective only if we actually use it.

---

[1] Go on now, give feedback a little hug.

Throughout this chapter, we will focus on what makes feedback effective and the factors that can get in the way of writers using the feedback they receive. Sometimes the factors relate to those who offer us criticism on our work—*feedback givers*, but often we're not aware that we—the *feedback receivers*—are the ones in our own way.

Not All Feedback Is Created Equal

Feedback can be one of the most powerful influences on learning (Hattie & Timperley, 2007), and few would disagree that feedback is essential to improving our writing. Effective feedback allows us to compare our performance to that which is expected and make gains on closing the gap.

However, not all feedback is equally effective. Feedback scholars characterize criticism in many ways, but two categories of note are evaluative and directive. Whereas evaluative feedback is past-oriented and focuses on what was done well or badly within the work, directive feedback is focused on the future and what can be done to improve the work. Of course, feedback can also be either positive (feels good) or negative (doesn't feel so good). Perhaps surprisingly, not all positive feedback is particularly effective or motivating and not all negative feedback is ineffective or demotivating. So, what ingredients might the magic feedback sauce include?

Just kidding. There isn't a perfect feedback recipe for every human in every situation. There is, however, quite a bit of evidence to suggest some basic ideas for improving feedback in many scenarios. In a recent meta-analysis of 78 studies exploring the effects of feedback on motivation, Fong et al., (2019) found that compared with positive, neutral, and negative feedback without instruction, negative feedback with instruction (directive feedback) had positive effects on motivation. Not surprisingly, negative feedback without instruction[2] reduced feedback receivers' motivation, and negative feedback with or without instruction had a negative effect on perceived competence (see Chapter 4 [Writing Self-efficacy] for more on the role feedback can play on our writing efficacy beliefs). However, evidence showed that receiving negative feedback had a positive effect on motivation when it was delivered in person, used noncontrolling language, and openly and honestly communicated high standards and potential.

---

[2] More of a feedslap than feedback.

Although across the studies positive feedback increased feedback receivers' motivation, it's essential for feedback to be genuine, because overpraising mediocre work can create mistrust between the feedback giver and receiver (Yeager et al., 2014).

So while feedback givers and receivers alike seem to prefer directive feedback because of its superior usefulness (Winstone et al. 2017), the effectiveness of feedback is nuanced by the feedback itself, the way in which it was sent, the way in which it was received, and the relationship between the giver and receiver. Among these complexities, writers have the most control over the ways they react to and use the feedback they receive.

Behavioral Reactions to Feedback

Receiving criticism about our hard work is never easy, really. Picture this: Lucy, your baby goat, is finally ready to show at the county fair. After months of daily training, grooming, and trimming, the big day is finally here and you can hardly contain your excitement. So much time and effort went in to caring for her and preparing for this moment—the moment for Lucy to be seen as the prized, gorgeous goat specimen that she is. And you, my friend, you feel like an actual goat whisperer because Lucy would not be this goat goddess without you.[3]

After rolling up to the fair, smelling all the smells, stepping in all the nasties, and getting Lucy to stand just so, you see the steely eyed judges approaching. They make it to your booth and you can tell by their expressions that they do not think Lucy is quite as remarkable as you do. You see them marking all the marks and you know it's not good. In the end, the scorecard clearly shows that you and the judges are not on the same page about Lucy's appearance and this news comes like a sledgehammer.

Now, let's for a moment pretend that Lucy is not a goat but instead is your prized piece of writing, perhaps your dissertation or a manuscript detailing some component of your life's work to date. What if you and Lucy get critical feedback that is unexpected, frustrating, disappointing, or all of the above? What do you do with it? Do you get a case of scrollitis, where you simply scan over the comments, only pausing to roll your eyes or sigh deeply? Perhaps you actively read the comments, but because you're

---

[3] Stay with me here, friends. I know it's getting a little weird, but I'm hoping it will come together in a bit.

so discredulous,[4] you decide to stop there. Or maybe you had a feeling all along that Lucy wasn't going to be perceived well so you devade[5] by refusing to even peek at the comments.

Research notes that levels of engagement with feedback can vary quite a lot from one person to the next (Caffarella & Barnett, 2000; Robinson et al., 2013). Of course, the healthiest and most productive response to criticism is to actively engage, make sense of the feedback, and use it to improve our work, but because of the garden variety of negative feels and the overall psychological experience of criticism, this isn't always possible (Winstone et al., 2017).

Emotional Reactions to Feedback

Going back to Lucy from the last section, receiving low scores on the dedicated caretaking of your prized goat would likely feel pretty horrible. Across settings, receiving criticism about our work can evoke strong emotional reactions, and reactions such as disappointment, frustration, shame, guilt, and embarrassment can lead to counterproductive behaviors and disengagement (Belschak & Den Hartog, 2009; Kluger & DeNisi, 1996). Emotions can also run high when we receive performance feedback about our writing (Fong et al., 2016, 2018a). Whereas honest praise can make us feel like we're walking on a cloud, criticism can feel destructive—despite the degree to which it's actually constructive.

Sometimes even the anticipation of receiving feedback about our work is enough to send us into a psychological black hole of worry and dread. In a recent study, we measured eye tracking and physiological responses during the writing process and there was a marked increase in participants' stress levels immediately after they learned they would receive feedback from their instructor on the essay they just wrote (DeBusk-Lane & Zumbrunn, 2019). I know that whenever I get the ping of an email with any indication that it includes some review of my work, I personally issue a silent prayer to the universe that the feedback isn't terrible. I've been in the publishing research game long enough to know that asking for the reviews to be overwhelmingly positive is laughable—academics, perhaps by both nature and training, are a fairly critical bunch.

---

[4] Discredulous = disappointed + incredulousness: *adj.* (of a person) shocked/confused by one's failure to understand something valued (Sher & Wertz, 2016).

[5] Devade = devastation + evade: *v.* to purposely avoid a situation because you're sure the outcome will be distressing (Sher & Wertz, 2016).

The feedback funk can hit pretty hard even when you're pretty sure that the person reviewing your work and giving you feedback is just trying to make your writing better, and they're not in fact some horrible demon not so secretly trying to suck your soul. However, our interpretations of the feedback given our goals, beliefs, and sensitivities, can make a difference in the emotions we feel in feedback situations (Lazarus, 1991; Pekrun, 2006). For example, Fong et al., (2019) found that shame was more likely to arise when participants blamed themselves for the negative writing feedback they received. On the other hand, anger was a more likely result when participants believed that negative feedback was attributed to external sources such as unhelpful feedback or feedback delivered negatively.

Your writing is so personal. They're your ideas. Your words. You. And when someone says your words are wrong, it can feel like you're the one who's wrong. However, a strong relationship with the person giving us criticism can buffer the blows of what otherwise might feel like a feedsmackdown.

Considering the Feedback Context

Giving and receiving feedback doesn't happen in a vacuum.[6] Instead, feedback is given and received within the context of a relationship and shaped by several interactions between the feedback giver and receiver. So many factors within this relationship can alter the ways in which we perceive—and use—the feedback we receive. Among these factors, care and trust are perhaps the most important (Carless, 2013).

We're much more likely to engage in feedback when it comes from someone who we believe is a credible authority (Stone & Heen, 2014). We might ask ourselves questions like *Just what are the chops of the person reviewing my work? Does the person understand the work and the standards of quality necessary for success?* It's also important that we believe the feedback giver is someone who understands our capabilities and is someone who we believe has our best interests at heart (Can & Walker, 2011; Fong et al., 2018b). We care a whole lot about our writing and success, so it makes sense that the value of our work is reciprocated by the person providing the feedback.

---

[6] It's probably good that giving and receiving feedback doesn't happen in a vacuum because the insides of vacuums are disgusting.

Equally important as our trust in the feedback giver is the belief that we are trusted to make appropriate decisions to progress our work. Such trust can be signaled through the communication of high standards and the tone of the feedback delivered. Our sense of autonomy throughout the writing process is essential and we're often more resistant to feedback that uses controlling language (e.g., "Change this word") than feedback suggestions that allow for autonomy (e.g., "Consider changing this word"). A subtle change in wording sometimes makes all the difference.

Feedback Roles: Whose Job Is It, Anyway?

When feedback goes wrong, we're often quick to identify why it went so wrong and point the finger at who's responsible. In one recent study asking feedback receivers how they might make better use of the suggestions and guidance they receive, 66% of those surveyed focused solely on the things feedback givers could do differently, such as ensuring that comments are more specific and detailed (Winstone & Nash, in press). Then, in the same study, nearly half of the feedback givers identified weak motivation or volition to be the single biggest factor preventing feedback receivers' effective use of their suggestions and guidance. It seems difficult for many of us to share the blame when and where feedback goes awry, and when learning and progress aren't, well, progressing.

In actuality, the process of feedback involves two primary players—the giver and the receiver—and both have critical roles to play. Whereas the giver provides opportunities for improvement, it is the receiver who must take advantage of those opportunities. The player to hold the power first is the feedback giver. It's the giver's responsibility to ensure that feedback is poised to guide the receiver's next steps. To be effective, feedback needs to be: (1) frequent, timely, respectful, and sufficiently detailed, (2) purposefully related to the task, (3) transparent and understandable, and (4) focused on learning and future improvement (Gibbs & Simpson, 2005). However, even the most helpful feedback can be lost on deaf ears if those ears belong to a human that is not motivated to digest and act upon it to progress the work (Fong et al., 2018b).[7] This is when the power and responsibility of feedback shifts from the giver to the receiver. Truly engaging in feedback requires that the receiver: (1) review and make sense

---

[7] All too often, I've treated the feedback that I've received on my writing the same way I did when I received wrapped socks and underwear as a gift as a child—with a fake smile and a "thanks."

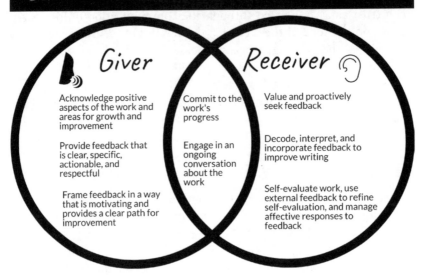

Figure 7.1 Feedback Roles

Giver

Acknowledge positive aspects of the work and areas for growth and improvement

Provide feedback that is clear, specific, actionable, and respectful

Frame feedback in a way that is motivating and provides a clear path for improvement

Commit to the work's progress

Engage in an ongoing conversation about the work

Receiver

Value and proactively seek feedback

Decode, interpret, and incorporate feedback to improve writing

Self-evaluate work, use external feedback to refine self-evaluation, and manage affective responses to feedback

of the feedback, (2) seek clarification as necessary, (3) select strategies to implement feedback, (4) critically self-evaluate their own work, and (5) manage any negative feelings, emotions, and attitudes that might arise as a result of receiving feedback and stand in the way of motivation and progress (Nash & Winstone, 2017). It's also important to note that effectively engaging in the feedback requires the receiver to not rush the process. Some welcome feedback but are reluctant to actually process it. When we receive feedback only to then process it on a surface level, we don't think deeply about the work to make it our own. Some call this the "just tell me what to do and I'll do it syndrome." To really learn and grow from feedback, we need to take time to digest the suggestions of the feedback giver.

Each of the feedback responsibilities aligned with the giver and receiver roles are illustrated in Figure 7.1. Here, it's critical to note that both the giver and the receiver have the shared responsibilities of committing to the work's progress and engaging in an ongoing conversation to see it forward (Carless, 2013; Hattie & Timperley, 2007). Without such commitment and dialogue, it's easy to see how learning, growth, and progress can be stalled.

TL;DR Summary

- Feedback can be a powerful influence on our writing, but it's only effective if we use it.

- There are a host of things that can stand in the way of our productive use of the feedback we receive about our writing.

- Directive feedback, or feedback that is focused on what can be done to improve the work, can be particularly helpful and motivating.

- From ignoring criticism altogether to actively engaging with feedback and using it to improve our work, people react to criticism in a variety of ways.

- Receiving criticism about our work can evoke strong emotions, which can lead to counterproductive behaviors and disengagement with the writing process.

- Feedback is given and received within the context of a relationship and shaped by several interactions between the feedback giver and receiver. Trust and care within the relationship are crucial components to the uptake of feedback.

- The effective use of feedback involves both the feedback giver and the feedback receiver. Whereas the role of the giver is to provide effective feedback, the role of the receiver is to actively seek and engage in the feedback process, and manage any negative affective responses that might arise during that process. Ongoing dialogue and commitment to the work lies on the shoulders of both the feedback giver and receiver.

Essential Strategies for Productive (and Sane) Writing

Waiting around for feedback that might never come or receiving negative criticism about our work can no doubt be difficult, but there are strategies for getting the effective feedback you deserve in ways that align with your needs and preferences. Choose one to two ideas from the following sections to begin.

Exemplars: The Hidden Feedback Source

What if I told you that low-risk (i.e., no human interaction necessary) feedback for your writing was freely available . . . if you're able to solve the mystery of where it's hiding. Rather than a twisted candle, an ivory charm, or an embellished jewelry box, the clue that unlocks this mystery is an exemplar.[8] That's right, you can avoid the dastardly peril of harsh writing feedback by sleuthing out expectations with exemplars. The definition of an exemplar is a quality piece of writing in a specific *genre*, written for a specific *audience* in a determined *outlet*.

The mystery within the mystery is to find the right exemplar, so let's break it down by the primary clue components: genre, audience, and outlet. For the first clue, determine the genre. For example, your project might be a graduate research thesis, a literature review, an empirical article, or a book proposal.

After cracking the genre code, you need to decide on your audience, your second clue. If you're writing a doctoral dissertation, then your audience is fairly given—it's, at least in part, your committee. However, if you're writing a journal article manuscript, then you will need to decide who you want to read the work when it's finished. Will it be for practitioners in the field? Researchers? Another group altogether? Deciding the audience up front is important, because this will set the style, tone, and content of your writing.

Once the primary components of genre and audience are determined, then you're ready to put the clues together to figure out the final clue of the finding exemplars mystery: the outlet. This is where your piece of writing will live out the rest of its days. An appropriate outlet will match both the genre and audience that you've already determined. For instance, if you are writing an empirical article on the elaborate mating rituals of male sparklemuffin spiders,[9] then you might search journals that have published similar articles on our eight-legged friends. A careful read of the mission/aims of the journal will also give you clues as to whether or not your audience aligns with the readership of the journal. After you've identified a potential outlet,[10] you can start your search for exemplars within that outlet. In general, the more recent the exemplar, the better, because

---

[8] It's a shame, really. Twisted candles, ivory charms, and embellished jewelry boxes are much more whimsical than exemplars.

[9] The sparklemuffin is real, y'all. And kind of amazing. Recently discovered in 2015, the male sparklemuffin spider busts some serious moves to impress the ladies. See for yourself at https://youtube/mq-r20mlGes.

[10] Or 2, or 3, or 4—I like to have backups in the event the first outlet doesn't work out. #Next

standards and viewpoints change over time. As a researcher in the social sciences, I often like to find two types of exemplars (if applicable): (1) content and (2) methodology. Whereas the content exemplar will match the key topics of the work (e.g., construct, theoretical framework, participants) as closely as possible, methodological exemplars align with the methods you used (e.g., structural equations modeling, case study). Be careful of red herring here, or available texts that seem high in quality, but are not. You'll have to use a critical eye to determine quality (e.g., rigor, prestige of journal, etc.).

With your exemplar(s) in hand, the plot thickens as you move to solving the final mystery of the case of the Hidden Feedback Source.[11] Cracking this case entails careful examination of each exemplar. As you read, take note of the headings, subheadings, language, section lengths, and level of detail throughout. These are the primary clues that you can use to self-evaluate your work. For example, if the introduction section in the exemplar is two single-spaced pages and yours is ten, then you either have some heavy revising to do or you need to find a new exemplar, outlet, or both.

From my dissertation to publishing for an audience or outlet that's new to me, I've found that the exemplars that I've sleuthed out like Nancy Drew are the perfect type of feedback needed to start writing in the right direction. Also, self-evaluating my work against standards in my field, methodology, or the publishing outlet helps me know that I've done what I can do on my own and that I'm ready for feedback from a mentor or peer.

Bravely Seeking Feedback

As referenced earlier, one important role of the feedback receiver is to engage in an ongoing conversation about the work with the feedback giver, and as a savvy writer, it's your job to seek the feedback you need. You heard me right—don't just sit around struggling in Writing Stuckville,[12] hoping and wishing help will magically appear. It usually doesn't. Like most things in life, if you want something, you might have to ask for it, and maybe work for it, too.

Now, how do you ask for this kind of support? Start with an email to your writing buddy or mentor (for more on finding mentors and other

---

[11] *Cue dark and twisty mystery music*
[12] One of the worst places to get a flat tire, really.

Box 7.1 Examples of Feedback-Seeking Questions

☐ Where in the draft am I on the right track?

☐ Is there a rubric or an exemplar that might get me started in the right direction?

☐ I'm interested in understanding what I need to do to make progress. Will you show me specific areas where I might improve and how?

☐ To continue improving as a writer, what approaches might I consider?

☐ Do you have any personal writing pet peeves that I might avoid?

☐ I'd like to meet in person to discuss your feedback. Is there a day and time that might work best for you?

supporters, see Chapter 8 [Finding Social Support for Writing]). If, when writing this email, you find yourself back in Stuckville, Box 7.1 shows a list of questions that you might include in your message. Of course, there are several different ways to ask for feedback, but the most important thing to include in your message—either implicitly or explicitly—is your desire to become a better writer. Directly asking for feedback relates to the #ExpectationManagement conversations discussed in Chapter 5 [Maladaptive Perfectionism]. Recall that the purpose of these discussions is to establish quality communication with your writing mentor, clarify the expectations that will guide your work, and maintain a clear path toward continuous improvement.

An important aspect of bravely seeking feedback is to prepare for the hard advice you could hear and how it might make you feel. Reminding yourself that it likely won't be all hearts and smiley emoticons *before* you open the email that contains the feedback about your writing might somewhat steel your nerves and help you remain open to seeing the criticism as helpful guidance rather than a personal attack.

Also, remember that journal rejection rates can vary widely in academic publishing. For example, the American Psychological Association (2018) reported that its top journals average a rejection rate of about 70% with some journals rejecting up to 90% of submissions. With that in mind, it's important to see the decision of "Revise and Resubmit (R&R)"

as a win. Though almost all R&R decisions come alongside a mass of criticism and suggestions for change, they also come with the opportunity to try again. Finally, don't let review delays derail you. I once had a journal article manuscript under initial review for nine months (!) and I had nearly forgotten about the paper by the time I received feedback. It likely varies by journal, discipline, person, etcetera, but unless stated upon submission, I typically mark my calendar for three months from the day I submitted. If I haven't yet received feedback by that date, then I reach out to the journal editor to inquire about the expected timeline.

Human Yet Strategic Feedback Management System

The steps of the Human Yet Strategic Feedback Management System highlight that while the feedback we receive about our writing can be painful because humans are emotional creatures, efficient progress is most likely to occur when we are strategic in our responses to that feedback. The steps should be followed in order and each step is equal in importance. When followed, the system gives you permission and space to react to the feedback, provides a framework for preparing to address the feedback in your work, and can help you prepare for a feedback discussion meeting or manuscript revision letter.

Step 1. Read the comments.

Step 2. Put the comments away—far away.[13] Let them rest in a place where you won't be able to see them for a while.

Step 3. Go on a walk, take several deep breaths, eat some chocolate, shake your fist toward the heavens, and rant about the ways in which your brilliance is severely unappreciated. Do whatever you need to do to manage any strong emotions you're feeling (see Chapter 9 [The Importance of Wellness and Self-Care] for more ideas).

Step 4. Set a calendar reminder (for a day, or five, or more) and distance yourself from the feedback until that day. If possible, try to avoid stewing about the comments during this time.

Step 5. Return to the comments. Create a revision spreadsheet with four columns. Figure 7.2 shows an example spreadsheet. In the first column, copy and paste each specific, actionable comment. I typically copy the comment exactly so that there is less of a chance that I misunderstand

---

[13] Like under your bed. Or in a hidden folder on your desktop. Or in a cardboard box buried in your backyard.

Figure 7.2 Example Revision Spreadsheet

Reviewer Comment	Plan to Address	Author Response to Include in Letter/Discussion	Location in Manuscript
Editor			
One major concern is that the literature reviewed is not always sufficiently explicated, nor is its connection to your work readily evident. Establishing how your work fits within the broader research in this area is critical for demonstrating its contribution.	Be very clear about connections across research and our project. Be very specific about how the findings of the studies described in Intro/Lit Review relate to our project	Thank you for this feedback. In this revision, we have taken care to clearly establish how this study fits within the literature reviewed. We believe this helps illustrate the contribution of this work.	pp. 4–7
Reviewer #1			
I think more effort should be put forth to describe and summarize the relationship between predictors and outcomes, both when discussing the previous findings and when discussing the findings of this study.	Describe relationship between each predictor and outcome more specifically. Provide examples and summary sections where appropriate.	Thank you for this feedback. We have described summarized the relationship between each predictor and writing outcome in greater detail, both within the introduction and when discussing our own findings.	pp. 6–8; pp. 28–32

the message. However, others find that rewriting each comment in their own words to helps them own the feedback in healthy ways. In the second column, write your plan for how you will address each comment. Consider what steps are needed to fully address the reviewer's concern. In the third column, draft a response that you could use in your letter accompanying your revised manuscript or what you might say in a meeting with the person who gave you the feedback. Finally, include page numbers in the fourth column so that reviewers can easily locate your revisions in the manuscript. Your revision spreadsheet might only include these columns, but it might also include others. For example, you might include a column that notes the specific tasks assigned to members on the author team/what you need from others. Another column could signal a rough timeline or the priority level for tackling each comment.

Step 6. Address the feedback one comment at a time. Zero in on where you can begin and remember to be realistic about what you can do with the time you set aside for writing each session (see Chapter 3 [Writing Stress and Anxiety] for more on planning).

Feedback on the Feedback

First, two surprises. Surprise number one: most academics do not receive training on how to provide feedback to others.[14] Because of this lack of training and complexity of the feedback process, not everyone (ahem, so very few people) knows how to give constructive feedback in a way that encourages individual writers.

Surprise number two: almost all feedback = ♥. The only types of feedback that don't qualify as love are sarcastic remarks or cruel criticism personally directed toward the writer rather than the writing. There's no place for feedback of this kind in the academy, because it does much more damage than good. The rest of feedback—the good, the bad, the clear, the vague, the positive, *even* the negative—definitely qualifies as love. I see you and your raised eyebrows with your *Whaaaaa?!* expression, but hear me out.

If you've never before given feedback on someone else's writing, then you need to know that it is not always easy to give. And it takes *a ton* of time.[15] That time is taken away from the feedback giver's zillions of other responsibilities, so criticism may be provided hurriedly or without the care that it deserves. As someone who often gives feedback on others' writing, I've learned that my criticism can sometimes seem overly harsh—not because I'm sadistic or mean or heartless or don't like the writer or that their work isn't good, but because I was pressed for time and wasn't as thoughtful as I perhaps needed to be.[16] Learning that a student perceived my feedback as callous was surprising at first. After all, I just spent several hours reading a draft with the sole intention of helping the writer improve, and I was annoyed at the clear underappreciation of my efforts.

However, listening to my students courageously share their experiences of receiving my feedback triggered memories of writing my master's thesis and receiving pages and pages[17] of criticism written in red felt-tip pen from my thesis adviser. I remember taking the feedback, revising the draft to the best of my ability, and resubmitting, only then to learn that he simply ran out of room for all of the criticism that he had for the original draft because the revised draft, too, came back dripping in red ink. Receiving that feedback was devastating and exhausting. Not for a single moment did I genuinely think,

---

[14] I know, considering some of the feedback you've received, you're likely not shocked at all.

[15] For real, if time could be weighed, it might actually weigh a metric ton.

[16] And, honestly, because of that whole lack of training thing.

[17] And pages and pages and pages and pages and pages. . .

Box 7.2 Statement-Starters for Feedback on the Feedback Discussions

☐ First, thank you for taking the time to provide feedback on my draft. I found [note specific feedback here] especially helpful. I also appreciated learning that I was on the right track with [reference praise provided here].

☐ Overall, I felt [note your honest feelings here] while reading your feedback because [note the reasons why you felt this way].

☐ In looking over the feedback, I have a few questions about your notes that I'd like to clarify [note areas in need of clarification here].

☐ I'm really interested in continuing to improve as a writer. Next time, will you [note specific things that might be particularly helpful the next time your mentor provides feedback].

"Oh, thank you. Thank you for these suggestions and for taking the time to help me improve as a writer." No, as the recipient of that feedback, I believe there was little gratitude, if any at all at the time. It was only several years later when I realized how much care and investment really goes into giving feedback—even feedback that is difficult to hear.[18]

These potential surprises and/or faulty assumptions are all the more reason for engaged and thoughtful (as possible) dialogue between feedback givers and receivers. As the feedback receiver, consider providing feedback on the feedback that you receive (Värlander, 2008). Don't consider this a license to reprimand, but rather a right to your feelings, as well as an opportunity to politely share your reactions to the feedback you received and why receiving that feedback made you feel the way you did. If you're stuck on what to say, Box 7.2 lists potential statement-starters you might use within your conversations with your writing buddy or mentor. Ideally,

---

[18] At which point, I emailed my former thesis adviser with a virtual Hallmark card and chocolates for enduring my terrible writing as a master's student and for helping me become a better writer.

these conversations happen face-to-face, because meaning and good intentions are sometimes lost in the text of written comments.

The suggested conversation starters implicitly and explicitly critique the critique, emphasizing ways that the feedback was both helpful and not helpful. Perhaps the feedback included specific examples that were (or weren't) especially clear. Or, maybe a particular suggestion provided an *aha* moment for you. The conversation starters also highlight the important role that emotions play in the writing—and the feedback—process. Again, the most important thing is that you're having the conversation in the first place, because these conversations help make the feedback process and the legitimate emotions associated with this process more transparent.[19]

Haters Gonna Hate: Keep Perspective

When you feel like you're drowning in criticism, it can be easy to lose track of the progress you're actually making along the way. However, tuning in to your fan club can help you keep perspective (see Chapter 8 [Finding Social Support for Writing] for more on building your support system). Make a list of the people in your fan club and consider keeping a box or desk drawer dedicated to housing the notes and kind words people say about you and your work. Having those notes nearby can help remind you of the people in your corner and the things that are going well on the really rough days.

And, while it's important to include peers who understand what you're going through in this club, you don't have to limit membership to your academic homies. Publishing research has been my job for a long time so seeing my work in print doesn't always seem like a very big deal, but because I am a first-generation college student, it seems like a big deal to my family. Admittedly, it's also kind of great to hear my little brother tell me how cool he thinks it is and that he's proud of me *blushes.* When criticism starts to degrade your sense of worth and the important work that you're doing, don't dismiss the kind words from your fan club. Instead, keep perspective by wrapping your arms around them like a snuggly, little puppy.[20]

---

[19] #ExpectationManagement for the win!

[20] You also might check out your local SPCA to snuggle an actual puppy when feedback really gets you down.

NEXT STEPS

- Give yourself feedback! Seek out exemplars by genre, audience, and outlet in order to map out expectations before seeking feedback from a mentor or peer. Examine the exemplars to self-evaluate the standards and writing in your work compared to similar work.

- Ask for the feedback you need from a writing buddy or mentor throughout the writing process. Be specific in the type of feedback you are seeking.

- Remind yourself before reading feedback that the comments won't be all positive and that it's being given to help, not as a personal attack.

- Acknowledge your emotions and the large part they play in receiving feedback.

- Separate yourself from the feedback: give yourself a few days, and then create a strategic plan to address each comment.

- Arrange a face-to-face meeting to give feedback on the feedback and create a space for more effective feedback and improved writing in the future.

- Keep the bigger picture in mind. Keep encouraging notes from fellow academics or your proud family or friends to remind yourself of your previous progress.

EXTRA RESOURCES

Goodson, P. (2016). *Becoming an academic writer: 50 exercises for paced, productive, and powerful writing.* SAGE Publications.

Hancock, G. R., Stapleton, L. M., & Mueller, R. O. (Eds.). (2018). *The reviewer's guide to quantitative methods in the social sciences.* Routledge.

Lovitts, B. E. (2007). *Making the implicit explicit: Creating performance expectations for the dissertation.* Stylus Publishing.

Stone, D., & Heen, S. (2015). *Thanks for the feedback: The science and art of receiving feedback well* (Vol. 36, No. 10). Penguin.

University of North Carolina at Chapel Hill Writing Center. (n.d.). *Editing and proofreading guide*. Retrieved from https://writingcenter.unc.edu/tips-and-tools/editing-and-proofreading/

HUMOR BREAK

Quiz: Which Animal Describes Your Openness to Receiving Feedback?[21]

Choose your favorite animal from the pictures below. Then read the descriptions to learn insight into the relationship between the animal kingdom and your level of openness to writing feedback.

Credit Line: iStockphoto.com/Sudowoodo, iStockphoto.com/CSA-Archive, iStockphoto.com/Naddiya, iStockphoto.com/bartamarabara, iStockphoto.com/Sudowoodo, iStockphoto.com/Galaxy

---

[21] Disclaimer: This quiz is ridiculous and in no way scientifically accurate.

Cat: Beholden to no one, you are aloof and detached from the criticism you receive about your writing. Negative feedback? "Fa-la-la," you say as you yawn and sashay away.

Raccoon: Curious and smart, you seek writing feedback with the same enthusiasm as a raccoon prying the lid off of a trash can containing chicken bones. Each comment is like the delicacy of a half-eaten animal bone.

Golden Retriever: Like the remarkable golden retriever, you are quite friendly and respond well to feedback. Eager for success, you learn new writing tricks with exceptional speed.

Bear: In the wild, you have a tendency to turn to aggression quickly and there are reports that you've occasionally attacked without reason. Your powerful jaws, sharp teeth, long claws, and proclivity for aggression makes others wary of providing you with feedback.

Bunny: Like a bunny spending its days in constant fear of being eaten, you're terrified of being eaten alive by writing criticism. High-strung, jumpy, and perpetually on high alert, you prefer to spend your days blissfully safe in an underground den.

Hedgehog: Using your prickles to defend yourself against the unwanted intrusion of harsh criticism, you roll yourself into a ball and snort at the mention of feedback.

Activity: Get It Out

Skip to the perforated pages at the end of the book. Then, fill in these speech bubbles with kind (or hateful, whatever) things to say to the people offering you feedback about your writing.

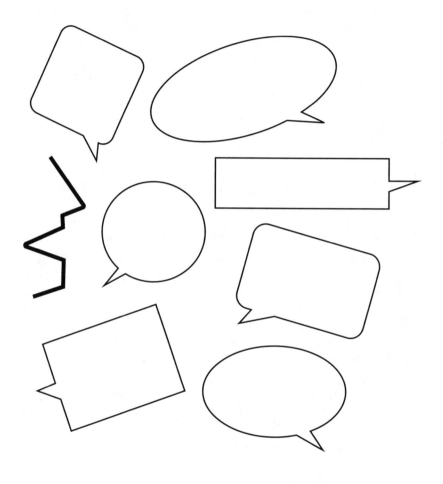

References

American Psychological Association. (2018). Summary report of Journal operations, 2017 and summary report of division Journal operations, 2017. *The American Psychologist, 73*(5), 683–684.

Belschak, F. D., & Den Hartog, D. N. (2009). Consequences of positive and negative feedback: The impact on emotions and extra-role behaviors. *Applied Psychology, 58*(2), 274–303. doi:10.1111/j.1464-0597.2008.00336.x

Caffarella, R. S., & Barnett, B. G. (2000). Teaching doctoral students to become scholarly writers: The importance of giving and receiving critiques. *Studies in Higher Education, 25*(1), 39–52. doi:10.1080/030750700116000

Can, G., & Walker, A. (2011). A model for doctoral students' perceptions and attitudes toward written feedback for academic writing. *Research in Higher Education, 52*(5), 508–536. doi:10.1007/s11162-010-9204-1

Carless, D. (2013). *Trust and its role in facilitating dialogic feedback.* In D. Boud & E. Molloy (Eds.), *Feedback in higher and professional education: Understanding it and doing it well* (pp. 100–113). Routledge.

DeBusk-Lane, M., & Zumbrunn, S. (2019). *Tracking eye-movements, physiological responses, and motivation during the writing process* [Unpublished manuscript].

Fong, C. J., Patall, E. A., Vasquez, A. C., & Stautberg, S. (2019). A meta-analysis of negative feedback on intrinsic motivation. *Educational Psychology Review, 31*(1), 121–162. doi:10.1007/s10648-018-9446-6

Fong, C. J., Schallert, D. L., Williams, K. M., Williamson, Z. H., Warner, J. R., Lin, S., & Kim, Y. W. (2018a). When feedback signals failure but offers hope for improvement: A process model of constructive criticism. *Thinking Skills and Creativity, 30*, 42–53. doi:10.1016/j.tsc.2018.02.014

Fong, C. J., Warner, J. R., Williams, K. M., Schallert, D. L., Chen, L.-H., Williamson, Z. H., & Lin, S. (2016). Deconstructing constructive criticism: The nature of academic emotions associated with constructive, positive, and negative feedback. *Learning and Individual Differences, 49*, 393–399. doi:10.1016/j.lindif.2016.05.019

Fong, C. J., Williams, K. M., Williamson, Z. H., Lin, S., Kim, Y. W., & Schallert, D. L. (2018b). "Inside out": Appraisals for achievement emotions from constructive, positive, and negative feedback on writing. *Motivation and Emotion, 42*(2), 236–257. doi:10.1007/s11031-017-9658-y

Gibbs, G., & Simpson, C. (2005). Conditions under which assessment supports students' learning. *Learning and Teaching in Higher Education, 1*, 3–31.

Hattie, J., & Timperley, H. (2007). The power of feedback. *Review of Educational Research, 77*(1), 81–112. doi:10.3102/003465430298487

Howell, J. L., & Shepperd, J. A. (2013). Behavioral obligation and information avoidance. *Annals of Behavioral Medicine, 45*(2), 258–263. doi:10.1007/s12160-012-9451-9

Kluger, A. N., & DeNisi, A. (1996). The effects of feedback interventions on performance: A historical review, a meta-analysis, and a preliminary feedback intervention theory. *Psychological Bulletin, 119*(2), 254–284. doi:10.1037/0033-2909.119.2.254

Lazarus, R. S. (1991). Progress on a cognitive-motivational-relational theory of emotion. *American Psychologist, 46*(8), 819–834. doi:10.1037/0003-066X.46.8.819

Nash, R. A., & Winstone, N. E. (2017). Responsibility-sharing in the giving and receiving of assessment feedback. *Frontiers in Psychology, 8,* 1519. doi:10.3389/fpsyg.2017.01519

Pekrun, R. (2006). The control-value theory of achievement emotions: Assumptions, corollaries, and implications for educational research and practice. *Educational Psychology Review, 18*(4), 315–341. doi:10.1007/s10648-006-9029-9

Robinson, S., Pope, D., & Holyoak, L. (2013). Can we meet their expectations? experiences and perceptions of feedback in first year undergraduate students. *Assessment & Evaluation in Higher Education, 38*(3), 260–272. doi:10.1080/02602938.2011.629291

Sher, E., & Wertz, J. (2016). *The emotionary: A dictionary of words that don't exist for feelings that do.* Razorbill.

Stone, D., & Heen, S. (2014). *Thanks for the feedback: The science and art of receiving feedback well (even when it is off base, unfair, poorly delivered, and frankly, you're not in the mood).* Penguin Books.

Värlander, S. (2008). The role of students' emotions in formal feedback situations. *Teaching in Higher Education, 13*(2), 145–156. doi:10.1080/13562510801923195

Winstone, N. E., & Nash, R. A. (in press). *Nurturing students' engagement with assessment feedback.* In M. Watts & H. Pedrosa-de-Jesus (Eds.), *Academic growth in higher education.* Sense.

Winstone, N. E., Nash, R. A., Rowntree, J., & Parker, M. (2017). 'It'd be useful, but I wouldn't use it': barriers to university students' feedback seeking and recipience. *Studies in Higher Education, 42*(11), 2026–2041. doi:10.1080/03075079.2015.1130032

Yeager, D. S., Purdie-Vaughns, V., Garcia, J., Apfel, N., Brzustoski, P., Master, A., Hessert, W. T., Williams, M. E., & Cohen, G. L. (2014). Breaking the cycle of mistrust: Wise interventions to provide critical feedback across the racial divide. *Journal of Experimental Psychology: General, 143*(2), 804–824. doi:10.1037/a0033906

Finding Social Support for Writing

One is the loneliest number.[1]

—Harry Nilsson

Understanding the Psychology

The writing process often entails seeking feedback, collaborating with others, and—at least most of the time—ultimately disseminating our work within public spheres. For involving so many people, writing can sometimes feel like a giant holy box of lonely. So often we find ourselves isolated in the ivory tower, sitting in our offices, alone with our thoughts, privately wrestling with ideas, trying to force them into words that will hopefully make sense to others. If you've ever felt lonely as an academic writer, then you're not, er, alone. One survey of university faculty and PhD Students in the UK found that nearly half of the academics reported isolation as a primary factor affecting their mental health (Guardian, 2014). Over time, perceptions of being socially isolated or feelings loneliness can take their toll on our bodies and our work. Studies have linked loneliness with fragmented sleep (Cacioppo et al., 2002a), lower daytime functioning (Hawkley et al., 2010), health risks (Cacioppo et al., 2002b), lower well-being (Heinrich & Gullone, 2006), decreased work performance (Ozcelik & Barsade, 2018), and burnout (Rogers et al., 2016).

Alongside our needs for autonomy (see Chapter 6 [Autonomy in Our Work and Writing]) and competence (see Chapter 4 [Writing Self-efficacy]), belonging or relatedness, defined as the universal need for social connectedness, is one of our basic psychological needs and central to our motivation, goal pursuit, performance, persistence, and well-being (Deci &

---

[1] You're probably singing that song inside your head now—sorry for the depressing earworm.

Ryan, 2012). As we've explored through the previous chapters, such things are important when it comes to our writing productivity. What is it that can get in our way of feeling connected in academia so that we can be our most productive selves?

Feelings of loneliness can stem from a host of different factors. It could be as simple as being physically distanced from others in your department or program. Personally, I live about 60 miles from my university office so I spend many days writing my heart out in my home office. My home office is lovely, but it's eerily quiet and as a raging extrovert[2] I often miss my colleagues and the academic chatter that fills the hallways at my university. Though physical distance from social connections is a factor for some, others might feel distanced despite their proximity to their colleagues, particularly if they find themselves within a negative psychological work environment (Wright, 2005). Social exclusion from professional interactions may especially affect underrepresented minorities on academic campuses (Settles et al., 2019).

Even if your workplace or program doesn't necessarily feel toxic, it's possible to feel like you don't belong. Perhaps you have trouble connecting with others because you're the oldest or youngest in your department or cohort, or maybe you're the only one with or without a partner or children, or perhaps you live a different lifestyle than your colleagues. Maybe you're socially reserved by nature and mustering the courage to reach out to others is daunting because even the slightest possibility of rejection is terrifying. Or, perhaps you have a mean case of FOMO,[3] but you feel pressured to *do all the things* and you're strapped for time, so instead of socializing over meals with others, your freezer is brimming with prepackaged dinners for one. Indeed, for many of us building a village might be easier said than done, but having people in your life who care about your well-being can bolster your feelings of belonging, decrease your sense of loneliness, and reduce stress (Reblin & Uchino, 2008).

The following sections explore the types of people whom you might consider inviting to your village and how those individuals might help you while they're there. We'll focus particularly on the relationships within academia linked to fostering writing productivity, such as mentors and peers (Kuyken et al., 2003). It should be noted, however, that supportive relationships outside of the ivory tower (e.g., family members, friends, therapists, counselors) can also provide support critical for well-being and success (Jairam & Kahl Jr.,

---

[2] I *really* love people. Being around people is kind of my jam. It's also important to note that loneliness isn't something that only extroverts feel—introverts get lonely, too.

[3] FOMO = Fear of Missing Out.

2012). For more on well-being and self-care, see the next chapter [The Importance of Wellness and Self-Care].

Everybody Needs a Mentor

Seriously, everybody needs a mentor. Even Oprah, Aristotle, and Luke Skywalker started their greatness with a mentor. In the wild jungles of academia and academic writing, a guide or two[4] might be particularly advantageous. Mentors can show us the way, answer our questions when we get lost, and provide much-needed encouragement when we fall along the path. In graduate school, faculty—especially advisers and dissertation chairs—naturally serve as guides, providing professional and emotional support (Barnes & Austin, 2009). Mentoring relationships may either be formal or informal. Whereas formal mentors may be identified by the department or university, informal mentoring relationships often emerge more organically when we connect with someone relatable who might be able to help us. Graduate students and faculty alike might benefit from a writing coach or consultant. Writing coaches are committed partners who can provide individualized support to improve both writing skill and our scholarly output (Baldwin & Chandler, 2002). Peers can also serve as mentors and help us move our writing along (Chai et al., 2019). I tend to refer to my peer mentors as "frentors" because they often provide both friendship and mentorship. The informal guidance provided by someone I can relate to on a similar level often not only normalizes my writing struggles but also helps me see a way to squash the struggles and maintain productivity.

Getting by With a Little Help From Our (Academic) Friends

Just as multiple mentors are likely needed for guidance across the various types of research and writing you will do over the course of your career, your peers and colleagues can support your productivity in many different ways, depending on the relationship (Jairam & Kahl Jr., 2012).

For many of us, our academic peers take a central role in providing the emotional, academic, and social support we need within academia. For me, I'm not sure I would have made it out of grad school without the

---

[4] Or 17. Or 35. One can never have too many mentors!

bonds[5] I created with other students in my program. As a first-generation college student, I didn't feel as if my family understood the new world of graduate school that I found myself in. It was difficult to explain to them that writing—and graduate school in general—can be really, really challenging. It seemed like the close academic friends whom I relied on were the only ones who actually knew what I was going through. They were the ones who encouraged me through my writing and publication woes, helped me navigate relationships with my other mentors, celebrated my writing wins, and provided the caring support I needed. They made me feel like I belonged because they understood and appreciated not only my nerdiness but my quirkiness, too.

As a faculty member, finding peers who understand and accept me as a scholar and committed colleague has continued to be an important component of my success. Over the years, I have found a couple of people who have been my ride or die colleagues, or the colleagues whom I call first when the going gets tough. These individuals are the ones I turn to first because they're often my collaborators. Honestly, the reverse is also true: my collaborators are often the ones I turn to first because they're often my closest colleagues. A mentor once told me, "Find people you like working with; then see what work you can get done together by finding ways you complement each other." This advice has served me well.

TL;DR Summary

- Belonging or relatedness, defined as the universal need for social connectedness, is one our basic psychological needs and central to our well-being and productivity.

- Feelings of isolation or loneliness can stem from a variety of factors, including physical distance, social exclusion, and differences among colleagues or peers.

- Supportive relationships bolster our sense of belonging and help reduce our perceptions of isolation.

- Mentors and peers can serve as important social connections in academia, providing both emotional and professional support.

---

[5] We (half-jokingly) refer to these bonds as "trauma-bonds," defined as the bonds forged amidst the sometimes semitraumatic experiences of graduate school.

Essential Strategies for Productive (and Sane) Writing

Feeling alone is the worst. Fortunately, research shows that supportive relationships can squash our lonely feels. Get to work by choosing one to two strategies from the following sections to start feeling more connected.

Inviting the Support You Need

The magical dreaminess of a village often doesn't happen overnight, but there are things you can do to get the support you need. Perhaps the first thing to do is believe that you don't have to do everything on your own. What would it be like knowing that a listening ear or encouraging words were only a text or office away? When writing (or perhaps not writing) is getting you down, you don't have to suffer alone. However, getting support means that you have to put yourself out there and be—or get—comfortable with vulnerability. Some of you might be thinking, "*Vulnerability?! Ack! No thanks!*" I hear you. Opening up to other humans can feel scary, so maybe start with just one human. One colleague or peer who might understand what you're going through because their work or life situation is similar to yours. You might be surprised that a tiny village of two can be a powerful game changer when it comes to social connection and well-being (Seppala et al., 2013). Once you've identified someone with village potential, ask that person to coffee. Or ask them for help—and accept help when it's offered to you. Social support comes in a variety of flavors (Vekkaila et al., 2018). Use Box 8.1 to consider which flavor suits you best right now.

If you're stuck on whom to invite to your village, then ask your adviser or department chair for assistance in identifying a formal or informal mentor. Or, you might ask a colleague or someone you trust to suggest someone who might meet your mentoring needs and be a good fit. Offering your help to others can also begin and sustain connections. No matter the connections you make, ensure that the people you've invited to your village are actually supportive. Only keep around those who add to your well-being or help you push your work forward.

Box 8.1 Examples of Social Support

- □ Socio-emotional Support: encouragement, trust, shared interests, and sense of belonging

- □ Co-constructional Support: someone with whom to discuss ideas and/or collaborate

- □ Informational Support: advice, expertise, guidance, and feedback

- □ Instrumental Support: time, materials, funding, networks

Ain't No Party Like a Writing Buddy Party[6]

Writing support groups come in all shapes and sizes. Many institutions and departments have writing groups, but you might find it beneficial to begin your own (which could be as big or small as you'd like). If you need quite a bit of support for your writing, you might consider a peer mentoring group. Within these groups, members meet regularly with others who are at a similar level of professional development to learn from one another, providing and receiving feedback and support. Findings across several studies show that participation in peer mentoring groups can have a positive effect on scholarly productivity, research collaboration, and peer support (Johnson et al., 2011; Lord et al., 2012). In a review showing the effectiveness of writing groups on academic publication rates, McGrail et al., (2006) found that group meeting elements typically are determined by individual groups and thus vary, but often groups met informally once or twice a month for one or two hours. Many groups incorporate peer review and feedback on writing content. Additionally, peer mentoring groups often hold discussions at their meetings. From encouraging peers through the publishing process to working on common goals, group discussion can span multiple topics.

---

[6] . . . 'Cuz a writing buddy don't stop. That's a lie. Writing buddy parties totally stop, but not until the buddies make progress on their projects.

Another type of group that also meets regularly and provides members support is an accountability writing group. Support in these groups typically comes in the form of establishing sustainable writing habits (Skarupski & Foucher, 2018). During each meeting, members share their writing goals, provide updates on the progress made since the last meeting, and discuss expected or endured challenges. I have found that the accountability group format helps me structure my schedule and keeps me on top of my writing goals.[7]

Whereas discussion is at the heart of both peer mentoring and accountability writing groups, members of communal writing groups might talk very little or even not at all. Communal writing groups offer a place for scholars to independently write alongside each other. Within my communal writing group, we meet regularly—sometimes daily—to write together. Many of the group members are in fields wildly different than my own, and all of them work or attend programs at a different university from my own. However, I have found so much comfort writing alongside these humans. Never reading each other's work, we simply write alone together. It seems that sitting next to another human who is struggling through the writing process in their own way for their own reasons can bring a great deal of comfort. Regardless of the type of group you choose, you might find that belonging to such a group has benefits of belonging to a community.

Virtual Support

What do you do if you want/need a writing buddy, but you're not exactly fit to be seen by the public because you'd prefer to stay in your sweatpants and avoid the shower altogether? What then? Perhaps you and your writing buddy have a no-judgment agreement by which you refrain from commenting upon each other's stench or tattered loungewear when you get together to write. Perhaps, though such kind and graceful writing partners are a rare breed. So until you find one, you might turn to finding a virtual writing buddy. The interwebs can also help those who aren't terribly social feel more connected. For example, one study found that while shy individuals had fewer "friends," they spent significantly more time on Facebook and had more positive attitudes toward their experiences on the platform than their non-shy peers (Orr et al., 2009).

---

[7] Or, say, feel pangs of guilt and public embarrassment when I don't meet my goals.

Sometimes, my virtual buddy is someone I know, whom I text to see if they're writing and if they would like to join me for a few virtual writing mini-block sessions (for more on mini-block sessions, see Chapter 3 [Writing Stress and Anxiety].[8] Other times I reach out to mostly strangers by posting a message to a writing group on social media. Together, we start a Google doc, video chat, or a thread within the social media page and write alone, but in the virtual company of others, taking brief breaks in between blocks of writing.

A quick search on the Internet machine will reveal that there is no shortage of virtual support for academic writers, both graduate students and faculty members alike. From coaches to groups and hashtags, scholars can find resources and encouragement. Perhaps the most comprehensive and individualized support comes from an academic writing coach. One popular organization focused on coaching scholars for success is the National Center for Faculty Development and Diversity (NCFDD). In addition to coaching programs, the NCFDD also offers writing boot camps and webinars for graduate students, post docs, and faculty.

Support is also available through several social media sites. Both the "Unstuck Academic Writers" and "Any Good Thing Writing Challenge" Facebook groups provide a platform for members to post questions and resources related to academic writing, and each is free to join. The Any Good Thing Writing Challenge group also runs a monthly writing accountability challenge for members.

Available on Twitter, @GradWriteSlack is a free graduate student writing support community. Members support one another through all phases of the thesis/dissertation process and have discussions on self-care, motivation, and other important topics relevant to the graduate student experience. For scholars who self-identify as first-generation students, @FirstGenDocs offers a virtual space for scholars to come together to discuss common challenges and successes. Each month, @FirstGenDocs hosts a virtual writing retreat for members to write alongside each other. In addition to these groups, useful academic writing hashtags on Twitter include #phdchat, #shutupandwrite, #acwri, and #amwriting.

---

[8] As I write this, I'm waiting for a reply from the following text to one of my faithful writing partners: "Yo! You writing this morning/in need of a virtual writing buddy? I needsta finish this chapter. #WritingWingman"

Escape to a Writing Retreat

This probably doesn't come as a surprise, but I *love* writing retreats. What's not to love?! The busyness of our day to day academic lives can make it feel like we have little time to write, but writing retreats force us to carve out time to devote *only* to writing, often in a lovely setting[9] and among other academic writers. Whereas some writing retreats are structured with time to write and time to discuss goals, progress, and challenges, other retreats offer the simplicity of a serene space for productivity. Writing retreats also vary in length. Longer retreats can last a week, while mini-retreats might only last a day. Some find virtual writing retreats to be more accessible while still offering support and space to write. No matter the format, many find that participating in a writing retreat provides a sense of community and enhances writing motivation and scholarly activity (Moore, 2003; Murray & Newton, 2009). The best news? You can create a magical writing retreat of your very own if you don't find an existing one that's affordable or perfect for you (for more on this, see Chapter 6 [Autonomy in Our Work and Writing]).

---

[9] Some of my favorite writing retreats have been at the beach, a cabin in the woods, or a vineyard. *nostalgic sigh*

NEXT STEPS

- Make a list of a few people who could become a part of your supportive village or who are already part of your village: formal mentors, informal mentors, peers, coaches. Ask one of them to coffee or for help.

- Offer to help someone who may be a potential village person to start a connection.

- Try out a writing group on your campus or within your department.

- As there are many types of writing groups, self-assess to decide what you want from your writing group and where you may find it: accountability or communal groups, virtual or in-person groups, meets frequently or only when needed, etc.

- Start your own writing group with just one or two friends at your favorite place or even virtually.

- Use social media and virtual groups to get accountability, comradery, or encouragement through hashtags, virtual support, or challenges.

- Attend or plan your own writing retreat.

EXTRA RESOURCES

Facebook: Unstuck Academic Writers Group

Facebook: Any Good Thing Monthly Writing Challenge (website: https://anygoodthing.com/agt-monthly-writing-challenge/)

National Center for Faculty Development and Diversity (website: https://www.facultydiversity.org)

Twitter: @GradWriteSlack (website: https://gradwritingslack.wixsite.com/gradwriteslack)

Twitter: @FirstGenDocs (website: http://www.firstgendocs.com)

Quiz: Which Disney Princess Is Your Ideal Writing Buddy?[10]

Complete the following quiz to reveal the princess destined to be your writing buddy.

1. What kind of feedback do you prefer?

   A. Only positive feedback for me, please, preferably in the form of a delightful song.
   B. Shoot me straight. I can take it.
   C. Feedback? Eesh. Please be gentle.

2. At a party, you are:

   A. Making new friends.
   B. Quietly sitting by yourself, thinking about work and wondering why you're at a party.
   C. Chatting with a small group of animals, I mean, friends.

3. What quality irks you the most in a colleague?

   A. Forcefulness
   B. Dishonesty
   C. Cruelty

4. What do you want most out of a writing buddy?

   A. All I need is someone—anyone—to write with me.
   B. My writing buddy needs to hold my feet to the fire, even if I get burned in the process.
   C. I need someone to read this mess of a draft and help me make it better.

───────────────

[10] Disclaimer: This quiz is ridiculous and in no way scientifically accurate.

MOSTLY A's: Snow White: Your ideal writing buddy is the "Fairest of Them All." With her inherent innocence, Snow White cannot see any evil in the world or in terrible writing. She therefore gives only charitable feedback on any writing she reviews. Friends with everyone, Snow White would love to write alongside you, the seven dwarfs, and all of the woodland creatures. She might even teach you how to whistle a charming tune while you work.

MOSTLY B's: Tiana: As a writer, you don't have time for dilly-dallying. You've got work to do and you need a writing buddy who understands that. Princess Tiana is a perfect match—in either human or frog form. Straightforward and incredibly focused, if Tiana catches you wasting time, she will promptly and convincingly help you kick your writing into high gear.

MOSTLY C's: Cinderella: Cinderella, kind to all, is your ideal writing buddy. She has faith in your writing and you should, too. Take Cinderella's advice, "If you keep on believing [in yourself as an academic writer], your wish [to be published] will come true [especially if you have a fairy godmother and some fantastically talented and creative mice friends]."

Activity: Writing Village Gallery Wall

Skip to the perforated pages at the end of the book. Then, use the frames below to draw the faces of the supportive peeps in your writing village (sure, you can add your cat, too).

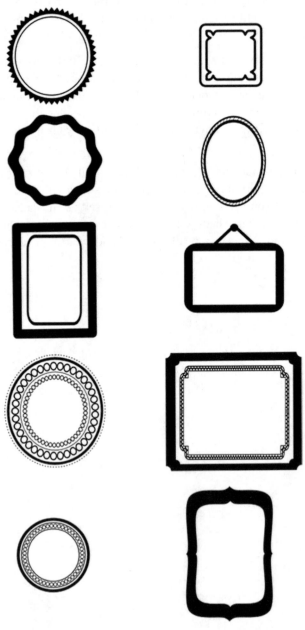

References

Baldwin, C., & Chandler, G. E. (2002). Improving faculty publication output: The role of a writing coach. *Journal of Professional Nursing*, *18*(1), 8–15. doi:10.1053/jpnu.2002.30896

Barnes, B. J., & Austin, A. E. (2009). The role of doctoral advisors: A look at advising from the advisor's perspective. *Innovative Higher Education*, *33*(5), 297–315. doi:10.1007/s10755-008-9084-x

Cacioppo, J. T., Hawkley, L. C., Berntson, G. G., Ernst, J. M., Gibbs, A. C., Stickgold, R., & Hobson, J. A. (2002a). Do lonely days invade the nights? Potential social modulation of sleep efficiency. *Psychological Science*, *13*(4), 384–387. doi:10.1111/j.0956-7976.2002.00469.x

Cacioppo, J. T., Hawkley, L. C., Crawford, L. E., Ernst, J. M., Burleson, M. H., Kowalewski, R. B., Malarkey, W. B., Van Cauter, E., & Berntson, G. G. (2002b). Loneliness and health: Potential mechanisms. *Psychosomatic Medicine*, *64*(3), 407–417. doi:10.1097/00006842-200205000-00005

Chai, P. R., Carreiro, S., Carey, J. L., Boyle, K. L., Chapman, B. P., & Boyer, E. W. (2019). Faculty member writing groups support productivity. *The Clinical Teacher*, *16*(6), 565–569. doi:10.1111/tct.12923

Deci, E. L., & Ryan, R. M. (2012). *Motivation, personality, and development within embedded social contexts: An overview of self-determination theory*. In R. M. Ryan (Ed.), *The Oxford handbook of human motivation* (pp. 85–107). Oxford University Press.

Guardian. (2014). Mental health in academia survey. https://static.guim.co.uk/ni/1399472932147/Mental-health-in-academia-s.pdf

Hawkley, L. C., Preacher, K. J., & Cacioppo, J. T. (2010). Loneliness impairs daytime functioning but not sleep duration. *Health Psychology*, *29*(2), 124–129. doi:10.1037/a0018646

Heinrich, L. M., & Gullone, E. (2006). The clinical significance of loneliness: A literature review. *Clinical Psychology Review*, *26*(6), 695–718. doi:10.1016/j.cpr.2006.04.002

Jairam, D., & Kahl Jr., D. H. (2012). Navigating the doctoral experience: The role of social support in successful degree completion. *International Journal of Doctoral Studies*, *7*(31), 311–329. doi:10.28945/1700

Johnson, K. S., Hastings, S. N., Purser, J. L., & Whitson, H. E. (2011). The junior faculty laboratory: An innovative model of peer mentoring. *Academic Medicine*, *86*(12), 1577–1582. doi:10.1097/ACM.0b013e31823595e8

Kuyken, W., Peters, E., Power, M. J., & Lavender, T. (2003). Trainee clinical psychologists' adaptation and professional functioning: A longitudinal study. *Clinical Psychology & Psychotherapy*, *10*(1), 41–54. doi:10.1002/cpp.350

Lord, J. A., Mourtzanos, E., McLaren, K., Murray, S. B., Kimmel, R. J., & Cowley, D. S. (2012). A peer mentoring group for junior clinician educators: Four years' experience.

Academic Medicine: Journal of the Association of American Medical Colleges, 87(3), 378–383. doi:10.1097/ACM.0b013e3182441615

McGrail, M. R., Rickard, C. M., & Jones, R. (2006). Publish or perish: A systematic review of interventions to increase academic publication rates. Higher Education Research & Development, 25(1), 19–35. doi:10.1080/07294360500453053

Moore, S. (2003). Writers' retreats for academics: Exploring and increasing the motivation to write. Journal of Further and Higher Education, 27(3), 333–342. doi:10.1080/0309877032000098734

Murray, R., & Newton, M. (2009). Writing retreat as structured intervention: Margin or mainstream? Higher Education Research & Development, 28(5), 541–553. doi:10.1080/07294360903154126

Orr, E. S., Sisic, M., Ross, C., Simmering, M. G., Arseneault, J. M., & Orr, R. R. (2009). The influence of shyness on the use of Facebook in an undergraduate sample. CyberPsychology & Behavior, 12(3), 337–340. doi:10.1089/cpb.2008.0214

Ozcelik, H., & Barsade, S. G. (2018). No employee an island: Workplace loneliness and job performance. Academy of Management Journal, 61(6), 2343–2366. doi:10.5465/amj.2015.1066

Reblin, M., & Uchino, B. N. (2008). Social and emotional support and its implication for health. Current Opinion in Psychiatry, 21(2), 201–205. doi:10.1097/YCO.0b013e3282f3ad89

Rogers, E., Polonijo, A. N., & Carpiano, R. M. (2016). Getting by with a little help from friends and colleagues: Testing how residents' social support networks affect loneliness and burnout. Canadian Family Physician, 62(11), e677–e683.

Seppala, E., Rossomando, T., & Doty, J. R. (2013). Social connection and compassion: Important predictors of health and well-being. Social Research: An International Quarterly, 80(2), 411–430.

Settles, I. H., Buchanan, N. T., & Dotson, K. (2019). Scrutinized but not recognized: (In)visibility and hypervisibility experiences of faculty of color. Journal of Vocational Behavior, 113, 62–74. doi:10.1016/j.jvb.2018.06.003

Skarupski, K. A., & Foucher, K. C. (2018). Writing accountability groups (WAGs): A tool to help junior faculty members build sustainable writing habits. The Journal of Faculty Development, 32(3), 47–54.

Vekkaila, J., Virtanen, V., Taina, J., & Pyhältö, K. (2018). The function of social support in engaging and disengaging experiences among post PhD researchers in STEM disciplines. Studies in Higher Education, 43(8), 1439–1453. doi:10.1080/03075079.2016.1259307

Wright, S. L. (2005). Organizational climate, social support and loneliness in the workplace. In N. M. Ashkansasy, W. J. Zerbe, & C. E. J. Hartel (Eds.), The effect of affect in organizational settings (pp. 123–142). Emerald Group Publishing Limited.

CHAPTER 9

The Importance of Wellness and Self-Care

Sometimes I give myself a break. So I will retreat a moment from the fray, just to breathe.

—Former First Lady Michelle Obama

Understanding the Psychology

Retreating from the fray can sometimes seem like an impossibility for academic writers. Fray is just there in all of its *frayiness,* following us around making it difficult to think or rest or breathe. The fray makes us exhausted. You know the type—the it's-only-today-and-I'm-already-feeling-tired-for-tomorrow type of exhausted. Across the chapters of this book, we've explored many of the challenges, pressures, and emotions that make up the fray and take our energy. But if we take care of ourselves, the fray has less of a chance to wear down our well-being and writing productivity. That's right, self-care is our secret weapon to escape the fray.[1]

Unfortunately, it turns out that there isn't a tremendous amount of research on self-care practices *specifically* for academic writers. However, there's quite a lot of evidence to suggest that wellness and self-care is critical for all humans—including those who learn and write about their learning for a living and especially those who wish to be productive. This chapter will review the science behind establishing and maintaining wellness and self-care in general and in your career so that you can be as productive as possible in your writing.

---

[1] Know what's better than secret weapons? Probably nothing. Secret weapons are amazing.

Why Wellness and Self-Care?

Wellness and self-care practices include several basic suggestions that you've likely heard from your doctor/parents/grandparents/fortune cookies: get enough sleep, eat nutritious foods, move your body, surround yourself with people who support you, be mindful about your thoughts, and be thoughtful about your work. These basic suggestions sound easy enough, sure. For many academics, however, engaging in self-care practices proves to be difficult to do with any sort of regularity (El-Ghoroury et al., 2012; Rosenzweig et al., 2003). This is unfortunate because practicing self-care can help grad students and faculty members be less-stressed and more productive in their work (Myers et al., 2012; Zahniser et al., 2017). In one study, graduate students experienced a significant reduction in stress after participating in self-care activities like restorative yoga (light stretching, deep breathing, and meditation), watching humorous videos, or reading articles about historical events and innovative technology for as little as 30 minutes (Rizzolo et al., 2009). Yet, occasionally might not be enough to reduce the stress related to academia. O'Neill et al., (2019) found that students experienced less stress only when they practiced self-care *daily* (no matter the type of self-care practice they chose) rather than weekly or monthly. So, which activities are worth adding to your daily routine? The next sections dig into the evidence behind specific types of self-care practice to help you decide.

Get Enough Sleep

A large body of research consistently shows the importance of sleep. Findings across this work suggest that sleep deprivation and fatigue harm your cognitive performance (Goldstein & Walker, 2014). In one study, researchers found that sleeping for only five hours per night for four consecutive days impaired performance to the same degree as having a blood alcohol content of 0.06 (Elmenhorst et al., 2009). Findings from another study showed that medical students who slept for five hours or less per night were more likely to report accidents or injuries and having made significant medical errors in their practice (Baldwin & Daugherty, 2004). So, if five hours isn't enough, just how much do we need?

The National Sleep Foundation recommends that adults aged 18–64 need seven to nine hours of sleep each night, but some may find that they need slightly less or more (Hirshkowitz et al., 2015). And, number of hours isn't the only thing that matters—quality of sleep matters, too. Disrupted sleep can alter our attention and our emotional reactivity (Medic et al.,

2017). Specifically, poor sleep can have a negative effect on our ability to understand and share others' feelings (Tempesta et al., 2018). Surely, it would be a shame if a tiff with a coauthor or the misinterpretation of feedback on a manuscript could have been avoided with a better night's rest. The good news? Some evidence suggests that if we lose out on sleep throughout the week, then it's possible to catch up on our zzzs over the weekend.[2]

Move Your Body

The list of benefits for exercise is rather lengthy. Among the assorted advantages, regular physical activity can regulate our moods and sleep (Dunn et al., 2005; Uchida et al., 2012) and improve our overall health and well-being (Penedo & Dahn, 2005). Although research suggests that exercise can decrease stress (Faulkner & Taylor, 2005), physical activity sometimes falls by the wayside during stressful times—when we may very well need it the most (Steptoe et al., 1996). Fortunately, taking just 10 minutes to walk around the block or having a private[3] dance party can be enough to instantly boost your energy and mood (Bossmann et al., 2013), and pushing for longer and/or more activity sessions can have additional benefits (Arem et al., 2015). So get out there and get a move on.

Surround Yourself With People Who Support You

Feelings of support and belongingness can buffer against the effects of stress to help us tackle our writing tasks (Kovach Clark et al., 2009) (see Chapter 8 [Finding Social Support for Writing] for more on building a supportive village). On the other hand, difficult relationships can add stress to our lives and make productivity especially challenging (Colligan & Higgins, 2006; Labianca & Brass, 2006). Worse, the number of difficult relationships we have in our lives at one time can exacerbate negative feelings (Venkataramani et al., 2013). One study of employees at a large life sciences company found that people with more negative relationships at work performed worse than their coworkers with positive relationships (Marineau et al., 2016). Academic writing can be stressful on its own—no one needs stressful people weighing them down even more. Minimize your negative ties as much as possible to help you focus on your priorities.

---

[2] Yay, naps. Naps, naps, naps. I heart naps.
[3] Or, not so private—you do you, buddy. Shake your tail feather.

Be Mindful of Your Thoughts

Remember Critical Cathy and Positive Patricia from Chapter 5 [Maladaptive Perfectionism]? How we talk to ourselves about our writing makes a big difference in how we approach writing tasks. In line with the self-fulfilling prophecy, our thoughts become our beliefs and our beliefs often become our realities. Practicing presence of mind can help keep our thoughts directed toward the positive and how we'd like to experience writing. This presence of mind is often referred to as mindfulness, or the nonjudgmental, present-moment awareness and engagement (Bishop et al., 2004). Mindfulness can also lower stress and improve well-being (Chiesa & Serretti, 2009). In a recent review, Lomas et al. (2017) found support for the positive impact of mindfulness on both well-being and performance in the workplace. Across the majority of studies reviewed, findings showed that mindfulness related to job satisfaction, professional quality of life, sleep quality, resilience, relationships, and professional competency. Research also suggests that we can get better at mindfulness by practicing (Goldin & Gross, 2010). Even better news? The positive effects of mindfulness practice can be achieved with relatively little effort. In one recent study, students who engaged in a 20-minute mindfulness practice of simple yoga postures and breathwork over the academic semester had lower levels of stress and maladaptive perfectionism and higher levels of self-compassion (Beck et al., 2017).

Self-compassion and mindfulness are often intertwined. One popular model of self-compassion includes three interacting components: self-kindness instead of self-judgment and criticism, humanity instead of isolation, and mindfulness instead of overidentification with painful thoughts and emotions (Neff & Germer, 2013). The self-kindness component relates to our ability to be gentle with ourselves—even amidst stressful times. When we practice self-kindness, we talk to ourselves the way we would a caring friend and resist judging our words or actions. What would Positive Patricia say to you in your darkest moments of writing? Don't let Critical Cathy come in and take over your writing self-care party.

With the second component, humanity, we recognize the hardships that we're experiencing are part of the human experience and not a sign that something is inherently wrong with us. We know that we're not the first (or the last) to struggle with writing or academia and this recognition helps us distance ourselves from the emotions of that struggle. When we practice this skill, we're also able to strengthen our empathy for others.

The final component of self-compassion is mindfulness, or our ability to be aware of our emotions without avoiding them or letting them consume us. One of the keys to the mindfulness component is to experience and feel that experience without judgment. We are able to recognize our feelings and acknowledge them without attaching meaning to them.

Let's consider an example of how the self-compassion components work together: You get the notice that a manuscript that you submitted for publication was rejected. You worked your tail off on that paper and thought it deserved a place in the journal. If you're practicing self-compassion–based mindfulness, you are able to slow down, take a breath, and notice what you are feeling about the rejection. You notice that you are feeling disappointment and sadness and you don't try to push the feelings away or resolve them. You simply let them be and allow yourself to feel them. You remind yourself that you are not alone in this experience—that others have also felt disappointment and sadness. This is part of being human. Your inner voice is not quick to criticize. Practicing self-kindness, you tell yourself that it's hard to feel disappointed and sad. You refrain from jumping to conclusions that you did anything wrong or that the editor or reviewers were unfair. You treat yourself with the kindness you deserve.

Be Thoughtful About Your Work

If you're a faculty member, then it's likely that you've heard (and felt) the phrase "publish or perish." Similarly, graduate students may feel overwhelmed with the gravity of finishing their theses before graduation slips through their fingers. These feelings of pressure are real, often intense, and accompanied by heightened stress levels (Miller et al., 2011). Whereas some academics enjoy working long hours to accommodate the pressure of productivity demands, others find themselves in conflict with the strain of academia (Hogan et al., 2014). Several large-scale and international studies point to job demands, job resources, and work–life conflict as primary stressors related to academics' lower well-being and feelings of exhaustion and burnout (Evans et al., 2018; Sabagh et al., 2018; Salimzadeh et al., 2017). Friends, burnout is bad. In addition to poor job satisfaction, burnout is significantly associated with health problems (Lomas et al., 2017; Zhong et al., 2009). Institutional climate and policies no doubt play a central role in our well-being and job satisfaction, and it's true that research and initiatives are sorely needed to develop proactive and preventative approaches to academics' psychological well-being (Duke et al., 2020). However, we must also take personal responsibility in protecting our well-being by aligning our time with our needs, values, and priorities (see Chapter 3 [Writing Stress and Anxiety] for guidance on goals and schedules). It's your job to take care of you.

TL;DR Summary

- #Truth: Practicing self-care is essential for peaceful progress and productivity.

- Engaging in self-care can significantly reduce stress and other layers of awfulness.

- We need between seven and nine hours of sleep to not feel strung out.

- Even short bouts of movement can boost our energy and mood.

- Difficult relationships rain on our well-being and productivity parade.

- Mindfulness and self-compassion can lower stress levels.

- Components of self-compassion include self-kindness instead of self-judgment and criticism, humanity instead of isolation, and mindfulness instead of overidentification with painful thoughts and emotions.

- Protect your well-being by aligning your time with your needs, values, and priorities.

Essential Strategies for Productive (and Sane) Writing

Dear reader, get your ears in here. You have to take care of yourself to be your most productive self.[4] Choose one to two ideas from the following sections to help you ride the emotional waves of writing with greater peace.

Get Your Good Sleep On

Fact: There are few things better than sweet, delicious sleep.[5] If you're not getting enough, then you might consider making a few changes. First, try to go to bed at the same time every night, because an irregular schedule has been linked with poor sleep quality (Kang & Chen, 2009). Next when you're getting ready to go to bed, try to limit caffeine, alcohol, and nicotine

---

[4] Seriously. No excuses.
[5] False. I mean, I don't actually believe it's false, but that's my opinion and not exactly a fact.

(Stepanski & Wyatt, 2003). Also, limit the use of your phone and other screens before bed (Eyvazlou et al., 2016). Exposure to blue light at bedtime can negatively affect sleep and circadian rhythm (Tosini et al., 2016). Finally, to ensure that your brain associates your bed with sleep, go to bed only when you're sleepy and avoid nonsleep activities in the bedroom (Vincent et al., 2008). Yes, Gina, this means not writing or working in your comfy bed. Track the differences you notice after making the changes. Do you sleep more soundly? Feel better the next day? Wake up with more energy for a productive writing day? Keep an eye on which changes make the biggest difference for you.

Find a Fitness Friend

For some of us, the list of benefits of physical self-care rivals the list of barriers standing in our way of actually exercising. Obstacles range from competing time demands and low motivation to a lack of self-regulation (Kwan & Faulkner, 2011). If any of these barriers ring true for you, you might try finding a movement buddy. One recent study found that participants who identified and exercised with a new sports companion had higher perceptions of emotional support and exercised more regularly[6] (Rackow et al., 2015). Your fitness friend could be anyone—a colleague, family member, actual friend, or even a stranger. Stumped on who might join you to shake it? There's an app for that! Try the Jaha app, which is like Tinder for fitness buddies. Also, check out the Exercise Friends site (www.exercisefriends.com) to find friends in your area who share your activity interests, skill level, and availability.

Mindful Social Media

Today social media is ubiquitous. Even my granny (who doesn't own a cell phone) has a Facebook account. Many of us use social networking sites as a way to idly pass the time or connect with our families, friends, and others. However, we should be mindful about how we engage online. A recent critical review by Verduyn et al. (2017) found strong evidence to suggest that people who passively used social networking (e.g., scrolling through newsfeeds) had lower well-being than people who used the sites actively (e.g., posting, sharing, commenting, direct messages). Whereas passive usage provoked social comparison and envy, active usage created

---

[6] Exercise + emotional support = self-care double whammy win!

feelings of connectedness. Avoid the dark side of social media by mindfully engaging in how you use it. That is, use sites to build your relationships and try not to compare your life to what you see others post online.[7] Or, take a break from social media and see how you feel. In one experiment, quitting Facebook for one week improved participants' life satisfaction and their emotions became more positive (Tromholt, 2016).

Mindfulness for Beginners

As academics, we're trained to pay attention. We scrutinize details of theories and our data to find greater understanding. But, for many of us, we forget to turn this thoughtful contemplation inward. When we pay close attention to our thoughts and experiences, we are able to see how the world around us affects our well-being and we're able to understand ourselves and our writing better.

If you're new to mindfulness and/or feel somewhat intimidated by the practice, then you might be relieved to learn that you don't need any special equipment, an overpriced aromatherapy candle, or a trip to India to learn the basics of mindfulness. You just need a minute. Literally, you need only 60 seconds. Well, 60 seconds and your lungs. A good place to start with mindfulness is to focus on your breath. Hundreds of physiological and psychological studies over the last several decades reveal that slow, deep breathing is associated with numerous benefits for our health and happiness (Russo et al., 2017).

For the next minute (or longer if you'd like), stop what you're doing and focus on your breath. Many practice mindful breathwork sitting cross-legged with their eyes closed, but you can literally practice anywhere in most any way you choose—at your desk, walking to your car, sitting in traffic, or during a rousing class or faculty meeting. For this minute, breathe more deeply than you usually do—try to exaggerate each inhale and exhale, and count your breaths as you go. With each exhale, try to relax your body a little more. Focus on each breath and notice how it flows in and out of your body. When you lose focus (everyone does—that's why it's called a practice)[8] and notice that your thoughts have turned to your grocery list or some random thought like why zebras have stripes, laugh it off and just go back to focusing on your breath. After the minute is up,

---

[7] Keep in mind that most people don't post pics of their failures.
[8] Attention is hard, people!

notice how you feel. If you have a smartwatch, check your heart rate before and after to see if there's a difference.

Set a calendar alarm and try this exercise at least once a day for the next two weeks.[9] It might feel weird at first (new things often do), but keep trying. You don't have to tell anyone that you're mindfully focusing on your breath, and they're likely to not notice unless you call attention to it.

Watch What You Eat

Decades of evidence showcase that what you eat can impact your physical health, but recent evidence suggests that what you eat can affect how you feel (Wahl et al., 2017). Specifically, loading up on fruits and vegetables can make you feel happier (Mujcic & J Oswald, 2016). Of course, other foods taste good, too. Some research shows that consuming a small portion of chocolate but eating it mindfully can increase positive affect (Meier et al., 2017). In one chocolate experiment by Arch et al. (2016), participants were randomly assigned to either the mindfulness condition or the distraction control condition. In the mindfulness condition, participants were told to focus their attention on the sensory experience of tasting the chocolate ("focus on the various sensations you experience such as the color, texture, scent, and flavor while tasting and fill your head with the details of these sensations . . ." p. 25). Designed to mimic everyday eating, participants in the distraction control condition were instructed to focus their attention on a hidden word puzzle while they snarfed their chocolate. Findings showed that mindfulness instructions resulted in higher enjoyment in tasting chocolate. The researchers found similar results in a follow-up study that replaced chocolate with raisins, often a less desired treat.[10] So, writers, make sure you're getting your daily dose of fruits and vegetables and make time for an occasional mindful minute with food you love.[11]

Strategic Agreements

What happened the last time you agreed to a collaborative writing project? Did the experience feed your soul and/or your CV? Was the collaborator productive and a good match for you? What about the last time you agreed to a service commitment? Did the amount of time it took align with how your work is evaluated? If when thinking about these experiences you wish you would have said "no," let that be a lesson.

---

[9] EVERYbody has a minute. Don't give me that.
[10] Valentine raisins, anyone?
[11] *Heads to the cupboard to mindfully get down on some delish chocolate.*

Box 9.1 Statement-Starters for Saying "No"

- ☐ Thank you for thinking of me for this opportunity! Can I take some time to think about it? I want to make sure I have the time to devote to being a good collaborator.

- ☐ This sounds like an exciting project. I'm really interested in your work and I'd like to collaborate, but I have several other irons in the fire right now and I'm not sure I'll be able to give it the time it deserves. Keep me in mind for future ideas?

- ☐ I can't. I'm simply at capacity for [writing projects/service commitments] right now.

There will always be more tasks than there are hours in the day so we must protect the time we know our writing projects deserve. Be deliberate when you say "yes" and intentional when you say "no."[12] Saying "no" is easier for some than it is for others. If you're someone who has a hard time saying "no," Box 9.1 lists potential statement-starters you might use to be more intentional and strategic with your agreements. Notice that the first statement-starter asks for more time to consider the opportunity. If possible, it's good practice to take time to weigh your options. Make a list of your priorities and time commitments to ensure that opportunities align before you say "yes."

Make Time for the Things That Feed You

Remember the schedule you set up for your writing goals in Chapter 3 [Writing Stress and Anxiety]? Well, it's time to make an important addition—time for you. #MeGoals—they're just as important as—if not more important than—your writing goals, and they are 100% not selfish. Tell your self-care guilt to kick rocks. *You deserve rest. You deserve to be well. Taking care of yourself is not a form of laziness.*[13] We can only be our best

---

[12] Otherwise known as "intention-no."

[13] Write those phrases down if you think you'll need to see them again in a few minutes/hours/days.

writing selves if we make time to be our best selves in the other aspects of our life.

Start by making a list of the things that make you happy. Your list can include everything large and small, free or pricey. Does the beach speak to your soul in an unspoken way? Put it on the list. Ever dreamed about rolling around in a field of lavender? Put it on the list. Does the thought of Ben & Jerry's Cherry Garcia or Thin & Crispy Pizza make your mouth water? Add it to the list. Is there a show, a friend, a hobby, or a special park that brings you joy? You guessed it, put them all on the list. Then think carefully about how you can make time for these essential pieces of happy. Start with one goal. Choose one thing on your list that seems reasonable to do at least once a week and put it on your calendar. If you're feeling pinched for time, schedule one short activity during one of your breaks (you can't work *all* 24 hours of the day). Don't know where to begin? Take a few minutes to go outside and look up at the sky or literally stop and smell the roses. Remember from Chapter 6 [Autonomy in Our Work and Writing] that even brief escapes outside can alleviate stress; the more nature-y the escape the better (Tyrväinen et al., 2014). At a minimum, include this protip from Ralph Waldo Emerson (1939, p. 438) as one of your #MeGoals:

> Finish each day and be done with it. You have done what you could. Some blunders and absurdities no doubt crept in; forget them as soon as you can. Tomorrow is a new day. You shall begin it serenely and with too high a spirit to be encumbered with your old nonsense.

NEXT STEPS ─────────────────────────────

☐ Track your sleep for a few nights. Are you getting seven to nine hours? Is it interrupted?

☐ Make some changes for better sleep and record how those changes affect your restedness, feelings, and writing progress (e.g., Go to bed at the same time and only when you're sleepy; limit caffeine, alcohol, nicotine, and mobile phone use before bed; and avoid nonsleep activities in the bedroom).

☐ Find a fitness buddy to help hold you accountable for regular physical exercise.

- Be aware of when you use social media passively. Instead, be mindful of when and how you use it.

- Consider a social media break. Take note of how it affects your mood and/or writing.

- Focus on your breathing for one minute, exaggerating each breath and relaxing your body with each exhale.

- Mind what you eat: make sure you're getting enough fruits and vegetables.

- Be strategic in your agreements. Say "no" to opportunities that don't align with your priorities and calendar.

- Carve out time for yourself to do activities and to reach goals that will make you happy (outside of your writing goals, which likely also will make you happy).

EXTRA RESOURCES

Harris, D., Warren, J., & Adler, C. (2017). *Meditation for fidgety skeptics*. Random House.

Moore, D. W. (2016). *The mindful writer*. Simon & Schuster.

Neff, K. D. (2011). *Self-compassion: Stop beating yourself up and leave insecurity behind*. Harper Collins.

HUMOR BREAK

Quiz: Test Your Self-Care IQ.[14]

Complete the following IQ test to determine just how savvy you are when it comes to self-care.

1. When was the last time you went out with friends?

   A. This week. Also, does brunch count as a friend? Brunch and I hang out every Sunday.
   B. Within the last month or so.
   C. I have fond memories of friendship. I was much younger then.

---

[14] Disclaimer: This quiz is ridiculous and in no way scientifically accurate.

2. How much do you typically sleep at night?

   A. More than seven hours. Beauty rest is kind of my jam.
   B. At least six hours.
   C. Must. Work. No time for sleep.

3. How many servings of fruits and vegetables do you usually get per day?

   A. The amount of fruits and vegetables I eat rivals that of a Brontosaurus.
   B. A few—especially if they're sneakily hiding in my food.
   C. Gross.

4. When you're stressed, you:

   A. Take a step back and breathe deeply.
   B. Take a walk around the block.
   C. Take my computer and throw it down the stairs.

5. How often do you make time for movement?

   A. Whether it's walking the dog, dancing, or axe throwing, I make time to move every day.
   B. Like Fergie, *I be up in the gym just working on my fitness* . . . at least a few times a week.
   C. My fingers move as I type on the keyboard. Does that count?

6. When new opportunities come your way, you:

   A. Push the pause button and think on it for a while.
   B. Usually say "yes." Saying "no" is HARD!
   C. Say "yes" right away. To all things. All the time.

7. Quick! Think of your favorite hobby!

   A. Eek! I can only choose one?!
   B. That's easy. It's _____.
   C. I used to have hobbies. Ah, the good ol' days.

MOSTLY A's: Self-Care Achievement: Unlocked! You are a skilled self-care ninja. You slay stress all day. POW! BAM! BOOM! Take that, stress!

MOSTLY B's: Self-Care Achievement: Progressing. You get that taking care of your body and beautiful brain is important, but this whole "adulting" thing gets in the way sometimes. Make a little more time for you.

MOSTLY C's: Self-Care Achievement: 404 ERROR. PAGE NOT FOUND. Yo, you might need an intervention. Drink four cups of chamomile tea, scream into a pillow, listen to nine hours of Tibetan singing bowls, and call me in the morning.

Activity: Self-Care Mad Libs

First, creatively complete the list of words. Then transfer your word list to the numbered blanks.

1. Adjective: _____

2. Plural noun: _____

3. Large number: _____

4. Bodily function: _____

5. Plural noun: _____

6. Food: _____

7. Strong adjective: _____

8. Animal: _____

9. Emotion: _____

Here are some of the 1. _____ phrases you might, perhaps, say during your first attempt at taking a hot yoga class as a form of self-care.

- "Get out of my way, 2. _____, I'm late for yoga!"

- "Is it me, or is it 3. _____ degrees in here?"

- "Something smells. Somebody must have 4. _____. Do people actually smell this bad?"

- "As I change positions, I start to see 5. _____. I'm either hallucinating or starting to faint. Or both."

- "I should have had 6. _____ for breakfast before taking a yoga class that begins with the word, 7. _____"

- "I'mma need more towels because I'm sweating like a 8. _____ in here."

- "I'm so 9. _____. Every time I downward dog, I literally start to waterboard myself."

References

Arch, J. J., Brown, K. W., Goodman, R. J., Della Porta, M. D., Kiken, L. G., & Tillman, S. (2016). Enjoying food without caloric cost: The impact of brief mindfulness on laboratory eating outcomes. *Behaviour Research and Therapy, 79*, 23–34. doi:10.1016/j.brat.2016.02.002

Arem, H., Moore, S. C., Patel, A., Hartge, P., Berrington de Gonzalez, A., Visvanathan, K., Campbell, P. T., Freedman, M., Weiderpass, E., Adami, H. O., Linet, M. S., Lee, I.-M., & Matthews, C. E. (2015). Leisure time physical activity and mortality: A detailed pooled analysis of the dose-response relationship. *JAMA Internal Medicine, 175*(6), 959–967. doi:10.1001/jamainternmed.2015.0533

Baldwin, D. C., & Daugherty, S. R. (2004). Sleep deprivation and fatigue in residency training: Results of a national survey of first- and second-year residents. *Sleep, 27*(2), 217–223. doi:10.1093/sleep/27.2.217

Beck, A. R., Verticchio, H., Seeman, S., Milliken, E., & Schaab, H. (2017). A mindfulness practice for communication sciences and disorders undergraduate and speech-language pathology graduate students: Effects on stress, self-compassion, and perfectionism. *American Journal of Speech-Language Pathology, 26*(3), 893–907. doi:10.1044/2017_AJSLP-16-0172

Bishop, S. R., Lau, M., Shapiro, S., Carlson, L., Anderson, N. D., Carmody, J., Segal, Z. V., Abbey, S., Speca, M., Velting, D., & Devins, G. (2004). Mindfulness: A proposed operational definition. *Clinical Psychology: Science and Practice, 11*(3), 230–241. doi:10.1093/clipsy.bph077

Bossmann, T., Kanning, M., Koudela-Hamila, S., Hey, S., & Ebner-Priemer, U. (2013). The association between short periods of everyday life activities and affective states: A replication study using ambulatory assessment. *Frontiers in Psychology, 4*, 102–109. doi:10.3389/fpsyg.2013.00102

Chiesa, A., & Serretti, A. (2009). Mindfulness-based stress reduction for stress management in healthy people: A review and meta-analysis. *The Journal of Alternative and Complementary Medicine, 15*(5), 593–600. doi:10.1089/acm.2008.0495

Colligan, T. W., & Higgins, E. M. (2006). Workplace stress: Etiology and consequences. *Journal of Workplace Behavioral Health, 21*(2), 89–97.

Duke, N. N., Gross, A., Moran, A., Hodsdon, J., Demirel, N., Osterholm, E., Sunni, M., & Pitt, M. B. (2020). Institutional factors associated with burnout among assistant professors. *Teaching and Learning in Medicine, 32*(1), 61–70. doi:10.1080/10401334.2019.1638263

Dunn, A. L., Trivedi, M. H., Kampert, J. B., Clark, C. G., & Chambliss, H. O. (2005). Exercise treatment for depression: Efficacy and dose response. *American Journal of Preventive Medicine, 28*(1), 1–8. doi:10.1016/j.amepre.2004.09.003

El-Ghoroury, N. H., Galper, D. I., Sawaqdeh, A., & Bufka, L. F. (2012). Stress, coping, and barriers to wellness among psychology graduate students. *Training and Education in Professional Psychology, 6*(2), 122–134 doi:10.1037/a0028768

Elmenhorst, D., Elmenhorst, E.M., Luks, N., Maass, H., Mueller, E.W., Vejvoda, M., Wenzel, J., & Samel, A. (2009). Performance impairment during four days partial sleep deprivation compared with the acute effects of alcohol and hypoxia. *Sleep Medicine*, *10*(2), 189–197. doi:10.1016/j.sleep.2007.12.003

Emerson, R. W. (1939). The letters of Ralph Waldo Emerson: In six volumes. Columbia University Press.

Evans, T. M., Bira, L., Gastelum, J. B., Weiss, L. T., & Vanderford, N. L. (2018). Evidence for a mental health crisis in graduate education. *Nature Biotechnology*, *36*(3), 282–284. doi:10.1038/nbt.4089

Eyvazlou, M., Zarei, E., Rahimi, A., & Abazari, M. (2016). Association between overuse of mobile phones on quality of sleep and general health among occupational health and safety students. *Chronobiology International*, *33*(3), 293–300. doi:10.3109/07420528.2015.1135933

Faulkner, G. E., & Taylor, A. H. (Eds.). (2005). *Exercise, health and mental health: Emerging relationships*. Routledge.

Goldin, P. R., & Gross, J. J. (2010). Effects of mindfulness-based stress reduction (MBSR) on emotion regulation in social anxiety disorder. *Emotion*, *10*(1), 83–91. doi:10.1037/a0018441

Goldstein, A. N., & Walker, M. P. (2014). The role of sleep in emotional brain function. *Annual Review of Clinical Psychology*, *10*, 679–708. doi:10.1146/annurev-clinpsy-032813-153716

Hirshkowitz, M., Whiton, K., Albert, S. M., Alessi, C., Bruni, O., DonCarlos, L., Hazen, N., Herman, J., Katz, E. S., Kheirandish-Gozal, L., Neubauer, D. N., O'Donnell, A. E., Ohayon, M., Peever, J., Rawding, R., Sachdeva, R. C., Setters, B., Vitiello, M. V., Ware, J. C., & Adams Hillard, P. J. (2015). National Sleep Foundation's sleep time duration recommendations: Methodology and results summary. *Sleep Health*, *1*(1), 40–43. doi:10.1016/j.sleh.2014.12.010

Hogan, V., Hogan, M., Hodgins, M., Kinman, G., & Bunting, B. (2014). An examination of gender differences in the impact of individual and organisational factors on work hours, work-life conflict and psychological strain in academics. *The Irish Journal of Psychology*, *35*(2-3), 133–150. doi:10.1080/03033910.2015.1011193

Kang, J.-H., & Chen, S.-C. (2009). Effects of an irregular bedtime schedule on sleep quality, daytime sleepiness, and fatigue among university students in Taiwan. *BMC Public Health*, *9*(1), 248–254. doi:10.1186/1471-2458-9-248

Kovach Clark, H., Murdock, N. L., & Koetting, K. (2009). Predicting burnout and career choice satisfaction in counseling psychology graduate students. *The Counseling Psychologist*, *37*(4), 580–606. doi:10.1177/0011000008319985

Kwan, M. Y., & Faulkner, G. E. (2011). Perceptions and barriers to physical activity during the transition to university. *American Journal of Health Studies*, *26*(2), 87–96.

Labianca, G., & Brass, D. J. (2006). Exploring the social ledger: Negative relationships and negative asymmetry in social networks in organizations. *Academy of Management Review, 31*(3), 596–614. doi:10.5465/amr.2006.21318920

Lomas, T., Medina, J. C., Ivtzan, I., Rupprecht, S., & Eiroa-Orosa, F. J. (2017). The impact of mindfulness on the wellbeing and performance of educators: A systematic review of the empirical literature. *Teaching and Teacher Education, 61*, 132–141. doi:10.1016/j.tate.2016.10.008

Marineau, J. E., Labianca, Giuseppe (Joe)., & Kane, G. C. (2016). Direct and indirect negative ties and individual performance. *Social Networks, 44*, 238–252. doi:10.1016/j.socnet.2015.09.003

Medic, G., Wille, M., & Hemels, M. E. (2017). Short- and long-term health consequences of sleep disruption. *Nature and Science of Sleep, 9*, 151–161. doi:10.2147/NSS.S134864

Meier, B. P., Noll, S. W., & Molokwu, O. J. (2017). The sweet life: The effect of mindful chocolate consumption on mood. *Appetite, 108*, 21–27. doi:10.1016/j.appet.2016.09.018

Miller, A. N., Taylor, S. G., & Bedeian, A. G. (2011). Publish or perish: Academic life as management faculty live it. *Career Development International, 16*(5), 422–445. doi:10.1108/13620431111167751

Mujcic, R., & J Oswald, A. (2016). Evolution of well-being and happiness after increases in consumption of fruit and vegetables. *American Journal of Public Health, 106*(8), 1504–1510. doi:10.2105/AJPH.2016.303260

Myers, S. B., Sweeney, A. C., Popick, V., Wesley, K., Bordfeld, A., & Fingerhut, R. (2012). Self-care practices and perceived stress levels among psychology graduate students. *Training and Education in Professional Psychology, 6*(1), 55–66. doi:10.1037/a0026534

Neff, K. D., & Germer, C. K. (2013). A pilot study and randomized controlled trial of the mindful self-compassion program. *Journal of Clinical Psychology, 69*(1), 28–44. doi:10.1002/jclp.21923

O'Neill, M., Yoder Slater, G., & Batt, D. (2019). Social work student self-care and academic stress. *Journal of Social Work Education, 55*(1), 141–152. doi:10.1080/10437797.2018.1491359

Penedo, F. J., & Dahn, J. R. (2005). Exercise and well-being: A review of mental and physical health benefits associated with physical activity. *Current Opinion in Psychiatry, 18*(2), 189–193. doi:10.1097/00001504-200503000-00013

Rackow, P., Scholz, U., & Hornung, R. (2015). Received social support and exercising: An intervention study to test the enabling hypothesis. *British Journal of Health Psychology, 20*(4), 763–776. doi:10.1111/bjhp.12139

Rizzolo, D., Zipp, G. P., Stiskal, D., & Simpkins, S. (2009). Stress management strategies for students: The immediate effects of yoga, humor, and reading on stress. *Journal of College Teaching & Learning, 6*(8), 79–88.

Rosenzweig, S., Reibel, D. K., Greeson, J. M., Brainard, G. C., & Hojat, M. (2003). Mindfulness-based stress reduction lowers psychological distress in medical students. *Teaching and Learning in Medicine*, 15(2), 88–92. doi:10.1207/S15328015TLM1502_03

Russo, M. A., Santarelli, D. M., & O'Rourke, D. (2017). The physiological effects of slow breathing in the healthy human. *Breathe*, 13(4), 298–309. doi:10.1183/20734735.009817

Sabagh, Z., Hall, N. C., & Saroyan, A. (2018). Antecedents, correlates and consequences of faculty burnout. *Educational Research*, 60(2), 131–156. doi:10.1080/00131881.2018.1461573

Salimzadeh, R., Saroyan, A., & Hall, N. C. (2017). Examining the factors impacting academics' psychological well-being: A review of research. *International Education Research*, 5(1), 13–44. doi:10.12735/ier.v5n1p13

Stepanski, E. J., & Wyatt, J. K. (2003). Use of sleep hygiene in the treatment of insomnia. *Sleep Medicine Reviews*, 7(3), 215–225. doi:10.1053/smrv.2001.0246

Steptoe, A., Wardle, J., Pollard, T. M., Canaan, L., & Davies, G. J. (1996). Stress, social support and health-related behavior: A study of smoking, alcohol consumption and physical exercise. *Journal of Psychosomatic Research*, 41(2), 171–180. doi:10.1016/0022-3999(96)00095-5

Tempesta, D., Socci, V., De Gennaro, L., & Ferrara, M. (2018). Sleep and emotional processing. *Sleep Medicine Reviews*, 40, 183–195. doi:10.1016/j.smrv.2017.12.005

Tosini, G., Ferguson, I., & Tsubota, K. (2016). Effects of blue light on the circadian system and eye physiology. *Molecular Vision*, 22, 61–72.

Tromholt, M. (2016). The Facebook experiment: Quitting Facebook leads to higher levels of well-being. *Cyberpsychology, Behavior, and Social Networking*, 19(11), 661–666. doi:10.1089/cyber.2016.0259

Tyrväinen, L., Ojala, A., Korpela, K., Lanki, T., Tsunetsugu, Y., & Kagawa, T. (2014). The influence of urban green environments on stress relief measures: A field experiment. *Journal of Environmental Psychology*, 38, 1–9. doi:10.1016/j.jenvp.2013.12.005

Uchida, S., Shioda, K., Morita, Y., Kubota, C., Ganeko, M., & Takeda, N. (2012). Exercise effects on sleep physiology. *Frontiers in Neurology*, 3(48), 1–5. doi:10.3389/fneur.2012.00048

Venkataramani, V., Labianca, G. J., & Grosser, T. (2013). Positive and negative workplace relationships, social satisfaction, and organizational attachment. *Journal of Applied Psychology*, 98(6), 1028–1039. doi:10.1037/a0034090

Verduyn, P., Ybarra, O., Résibois, M., Jonides, J., & Kross, E. (2017). Do social network sites enhance or undermine subjective well-being? A critical review. *Social Issues and Policy Review*, 11(1), 274–302. doi:10.1111/sipr.12033

Vincent, N., Lewycky, S., & Finnegan, H. (2008). Barriers to engagement in sleep restriction and stimulus control in chronic insomnia. *Journal of Consulting and Clinical Psychology, 76*(5), 820–828. doi:10.1037/0022-006X.76.5.820

Wahl, D. R., Villinger, K., König, L. M., Ziesemer, K., Schupp, H. T., & Renner, B. (2017). Healthy food choices are happy food choices: Evidence from a real life sample using smartphone based assessments. *Scientific Reports, 7*(1), 1–8. doi:10.1038/s41598-017-17262-9

Zahniser, E., Rupert, P. A., & Dorociak, K. E. (2017). Self-Care in clinical psychology graduate training. *Training and Education in Professional Psychology, 11*(4), 283–289. doi:10.1037/tep0000172

Zhong, J., You, J., Gan, Y., Zhang, Y., Lu, C., & Wang, H. (2009). Job stress, burnout, depression symptoms, and physical health among Chinese university teachers. *Psychological Reports, 105*(3 Pt 2), 1248–1254. doi:10.2466/PR0.105.F.1248-1254

Afterword: An (Un)Ending of Sorts

Maybe everything comes out all right, if you keep on trying. Anyway, you have to keep on trying; nothing will come out right if you don't.

—Laura Ingalls Wilder

Friends, by writing this book and dissecting the psychological and emotional hurdles of academic writing, everything has indeed, come out all right. I'm pleased to share that I have successfully defeated all of my writing neuroses. Words and ideas now come to me so effortlessly. As a matter of fact, writing is now my greatest joy. I love sitting at my computer hammering out words all day, every single day.

Confession: That whole last bit is an absurd lie. Writing is totally not my favorite thing. It sometimes still makes me sweat. It sometimes still ties my brain in knots. And sometimes, I totally still avoid it when it feels too big or too important or too everything.[1] So, it seems as though my writing neuroses haven't completely disappeared after all. Admittedly, that's rather disappointing. I *kinda* hoped that through researching and writing this book I *might* be cured from the shenanigans my writing brain happens to be riddled with. I guess I had these hopes because that's what people who write books about writing are supposed be like, right? Well, either I'm some bewildering outlier or I'm simply normal (er, not normal like a *normal* person, obviously, but normal in my struggles with writing). After reading far too many books about writing, it turns out that I'm not alone. Writing is *really hard* . . . even for writers who research and write about writing.

If you, too, struggle with writing and find yourself deep in the funk of all the feels *even* after reading this book and trying all the strategies, remember that the work needed to be a better and more peaceful academic writer is ongoing. And because that work is ongoing, I'll probably see you again. Be gentle with yourself and come back to the lessons and strategies in this book as often as you need as you keep trying—everything might very well come out all right.

For now, I have to scoot. Now that I've finished this manuscript, I'm off to the store to buy cupcakes for my "Manuscript Birthday Party" that I'm hosting tonight. It's time for you to put this book down and get back to your writing so that you, too, can throw birthday parties for your manuscripts.

---

[1] True story: To help me meet the deadline of writing the final part of this book, I bought five (five!) bird feeders to place outside my office window so that the birds could keep me company and keep my booty in my writing chair. It's like a raging aviary out there, y'all.

Tear-out Section: Chapter Activities

Activity: Put Your Grace Goggles On!
Activity: Dress Your Writing Monster
Activity: A Choose-Your-Own Writing Self-Efficacy Adventure
Activity: Perfectionism Voodoo Doll
Activity: Things-You-Can-Control Coloring Page
Activity: Get It Out
Activity: Writing Village Gallery Wall
A Final Activity: A Writing Shenanigans Maze

Activity: Put Your Grace Goggles On!

Within the grace goggles lenses below, write one statement that will help you remember the grace you need and deserve on your journey to becoming a more peaceful academic writer. Then, cut these bad boys out and keep your grace statement in sight while you write.

Credit Line: iStockphoto.com/adekvat

Activity: Dress Your Writing Monster

Cut out the pictures to transform your personal Writing Monster (add color for extra effect). Turns out that a Hawaiian shirt, cargo shorts, and a pair of shades can turn even the most menacing of beasts into a charming beach creature (who knew?!).

Activity: A Choose-Your-Own Writing Self-Efficacy Adventure
SO YOU WANT TO BE AN ACADEMIC WRITER?

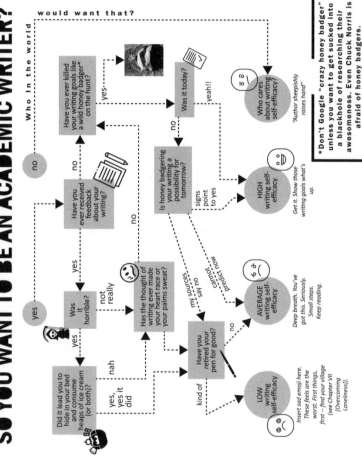

Credit Line: iStock/Sudowoodo, iStock/Amornism, iStock/bsd555, iStock/Penti-Stock, iStock/Freder, iStock/Gunay Abdullayeva

Activity: Perfectionism Voodoo Doll

This voodoo doll will repel the negative energies of your perfectionism. After cutting out the doll, simply use thumbtacks or draw pins to prick your perfectionistic tendencies that need repelling.

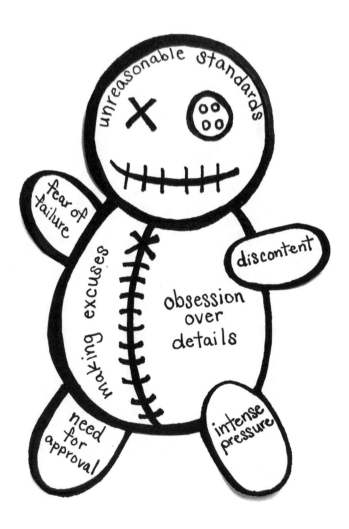

Activity: Things-You-Can-Control Coloring Page

Shade the images that you have control over.

how you spend
your time

the temperature
in your office

your computer

your writing

you (*hint: you're
already shaded!*)

where you work

saving your work

father time

your pen

your cat

your collaborators

rush-hour traffic

Activity: Get It Out

Fill in these speech bubbles with kind (or hateful, whatever) things to say to the people offering you feedback about your writing.

Activity: Writing Village Gallery Wall

Use the frames to draw the faces of the supportive peeps in your writing village (sure, you can add your cat, too).

A Final Activity: A Writing Shenanigans Maze

AVOID THE DEADLY TRAPS!

TRAP 1
Imposter
Quicksand

TRAP 2
Low Self-Efficacy
Tornado Alley

TRAP 3
Fire Pit
of Anxiety

TRAP 4
Critical Cathy's
Dragon Lair

Make it through the maze to defeat some of the most treacherous writing shenanigans!

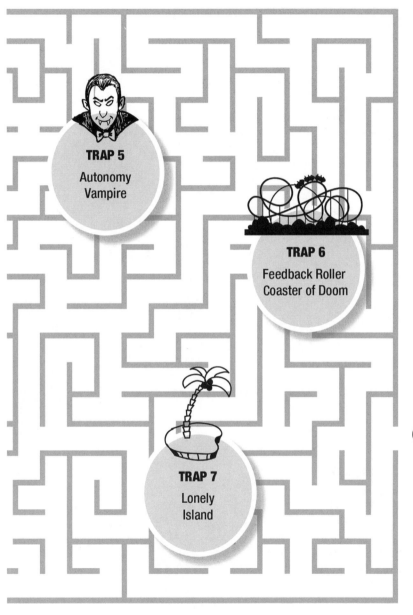

TRAP 5
Autonomy
Vampire

TRAP 6
Feedback Roller
Coaster of Doom

TRAP 7
Lonely
Island

Progress

NOTES

NOTES